COMMUNION THOUGHTS.

BY

S. G. BULFINCH,

AUTHOR OF "LAYS OF THE GOSPEL."

"O thou true Eastern Star!
Saviour! atoning Lord! where'er we roam,
Draw still our hearts to thee, else, else how vain
Their hope, the fair lost birthright to regain!"
MRS. HEMANS.

THIRD EDITION.

BOSTON:
WALKER, WISE, & CO.,
245 WASHINGTON STREET.
1860.

ADVERTISEMENT.

THERE are many in our congregations, who are withheld from participating in the communion, by causes which a fair consideration of the subject would be likely to remove. There are others, probably, who unite in the ordinance from a sense of duty, but to whom it is not as interesting and improving as it ought to be, through the difficulty of directing the current of the thoughts, and developing the religious feelings. This little volume is an attempt to meet, in some humble degree, the spiritual wants of these two classes. It is composed of materials, in part written for the purpose, and in part prepared for the pulpit in the course of the author's ministry. A few pieces in verse are inserted, none of which have before been published.

CONTENTS.

PART I.

THE LORD'S SUPPER.

PART II.

OUR SAVIOUR.

PART III.

THE COMMUNICANT.

PART IV.

THE CHRISTIAN'S WALK.

PART V.

MEDITATIONS IN VERSE.

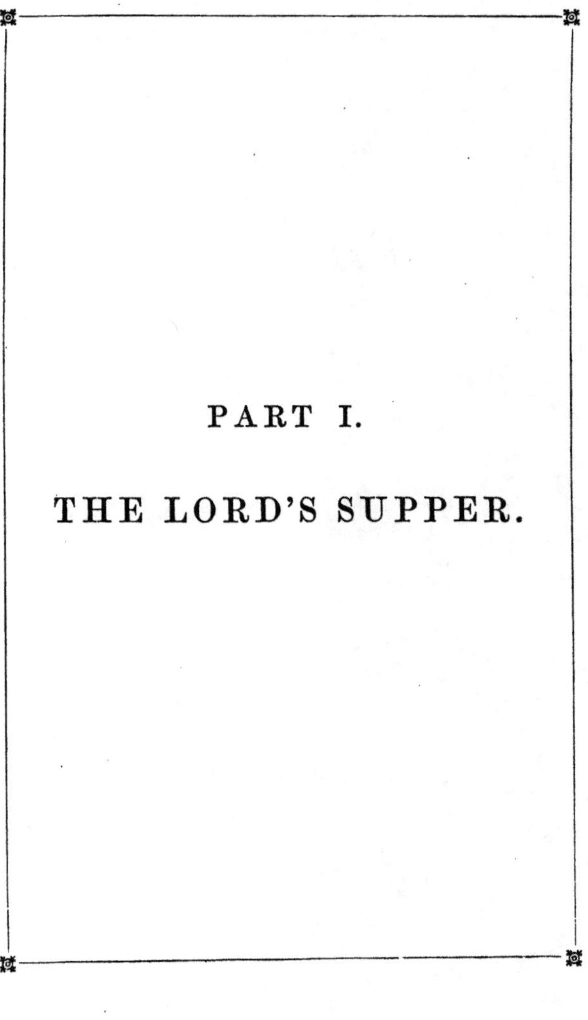

PART I.

THE LORD'S SUPPER.

PART I.

THE LORD'S SUPPER.

VALUE OF OUTWARD FORMS.

THERE exists, in the present age, an increasing indifference to outward forms in religion. Men have so long groaned under the bondage of observances, that a reaction has taken place. Becoming aware of the fact, that mere forms are not truth and right, men have begun to show a disposition to reject them altogether; and numbers, viewing the Christian ordinances as mere forms, have so far undervalued them, as entirely to neglect participation in their important advantages.

A well-judging mind, however, will look with some degree of suspicion upon any thing so transient and uncertain as the spirit of the age. We must not suffer ourselves to be hurried along by the influence of the opinions which happen for the time to be prevalent. We have the Scriptures before us, we have reason within us. Relying on these, and on the Divine blessing, let us decide whether we shall do well to discard or to neglect institutions which are hallowed, not only by the observance of eighteen centuries, but by the original appointment of our Saviour, and by the exercise of a most blessed and useful influence over those who engage in them aright.

Man is an intellectual, a spiritual being. But this spiritual being is also corporeal; this intellectual being can receive impressions from an earthly source, only through the medium of the outward senses. Whatever is to be addressed to man, with the design to affect his conduct and character, must be adapted to both portions of his compound nature. It must be suited to influence his thoughts and feelings, but it cannot reach these except through the avenues of sight and hearing; to these faculties, also, it must be adapted. Religion, though in itself a spiritual thing, cannot dispense with external means for its communication and development. Among these external means various services and ceremonies have from time to time been employed. One of them was sacrifice, so generally practised throughout the world in ancient times. Another was fasting, an outward expression of sorrow, designed to promote the feeling of self-condemnation from which that sorrow resulted. We may find another in that solemn music, which is employed among ourselves, as it has been for ages, to assist the devotional tendency of the mind. Nor are these the only external services. Preaching is external; however it may be addressed to the intellect or the heart, it can reach these only through an outward sense. Prayer is external, — all prayer that is uttered in words. Nay, even that which, without utterance, assumes the form of words within the mind, partakes of the outward and of the ceremonial. The Society of Friends, carefully as they have endeavoured to avoid formalism, have not been able to dispense with forms. The assembling together is an outward form; the signal for separation is given by a simple but expressive form; and the solemn stillness of the assembly while engaged in worship is valued for precisely the same reason for which the Catholic values the rich music that accompanies and aids his aspirations.

Must we, then, on the ground that religion ought to be spiritual, give up at once all that is external, and, classing together the ancient sacrifice, the modern liturgy, and public and private prayers, of whatever kind, resolve to be religious only in the secret feelings of the heart? Thus doing, we should act inconsistently with our nature, for we should forget its compound character. We are not exclusively spiritual beings. In us, dwelling in these material tabernacles, the secret feelings of the heart need prompting and encouragement by something external to themselves. We have, then, only one course left, worthy of our adoption. That course is, to make use of outward means, not as though religion consisted in them, but that we may become more successful in the attainment of our ultimate object, the true religious character.

THE PLEDGE OF CHRISTIAN DUTY.

We have witnessed, of late years, a surprising movement in the community on a subject of moral reform. The progress of intemperance, which had produced the most fearful ravages in our own and in other lands, has been arrested. Thousands have been rescued, who, but for this movement, would have gone down to a dishonored grave. The means for the accomplishment of this great good was simple. It was a pledge, a bond of union. It was the practical adoption of the idea, that those who had firmness enough for the purpose should come out and profess themselves friends of temperance, — friends of temperance in opinion, and resolved to be friends of temperance in practice. What that pledge was to this branch of moral reform, is the communion of the Lord's Supper to Christianity. It is the pledge of belief and of obedience. It is the outward sign by which the individual declares that he has taken his side in the struggle between good and evil in the world; that he has chosen his place, humbly, indeed, but with calm faith and hope, at the feet of his Redeemer, and in the company of that Redeemer's followers.

If, then, we have seen — and who has not? — the effect produced for the amelioration of character by the adoption of the pledge of temperance, may we not expect results corresponding in importance from the voluntary assumption of that which is the pledge of abstinence from *all* evil? He who meets his fellow-Christians at the table of the Lord has, indeed, contracted no new obligations; but he has avowed those which already existed, and has thus strengthened their influence over him. That which was innocent for him previously, is innocent still; but he now feels that more is dependent on the correctness of his conduct than before. He is surrounded with a cloud of witnesses. The community at large, his brethren in the fellowship of Christ, his own aspirations of piety and resolutions of virtue, all warn him against remissness, and exhort him to perseverance. Let it not be said that the responsibleness is too heavy to be assumed. We scruple not, when called by circumstances to any station which we are competent to fill, to pledge ourselves to the due performance of its duties. We intend to be faithful, and it occurs not to us that any danger is incurred by professing that intention. Why, then, if we intend to be faithful to God, and Christ, and our own souls, should we scruple to avow that intention by what our religion has made its appropriate pledge? Why should we anticipate a desertion of duty which is far from our purpose, and against which the very profession we are called to make will aid in securing us?

WHO IS ON THE LORD'S SIDE?

We learn, from the account in the book of Exodus, that while the lawgiver of the Israelites was on the height of Sinai, holding sublime intercourse with the Almighty, the people, weary with the long tarrying of their leader, were urged by their impatience into crime. In imitation of the idolatry of their Egyptian masters, they made a calf of gold, and consecrated it as an emblem of Jehovah. They evidently had no thought of relinquishing the service of the Being who had brought them out of the land of Egypt, yet their worship of him, by means of this unworthy image, was in direct violation of the command he had given them, and was justly regarded as an act of treason and idolatry. They proclaimed a feast unto the Lord, and, assembling around the idol which their hands had made, they "sat down to eat and to drink, and rose up to play." In the midst of their presumptuous worship and indecorous mirth, Moses appeared, accompanied only by his attendant, Joshua, but in the strength of indomitable courage, of a holy purpose, and of conscious intercourse with God. Dashing from his hands, in the excitement of the moment, the sacred tables of the law which he bore, he commanded the instant destruction of the idol. But this was not enough. Far and wide around, he saw the people scattered in shameful revelry, exposed without defence to the sudden incursion of any enemy, and yet evidently disposed to resist his authority. "Who is on the Lord's side?" he exclaimed; "let him come unto me." Among the twelve tribes, only his own, that of Levi, gathered at the summons. He sent them forth, with a severity which the extent of the defection rendered necessary, to punish those who persevered in their idolatry; but only by the death of three thousand of the rebels were the people reduced to penitence and submission.

"Who is on the Lord's side?" That dread summons, which then rang through the disordered camp of Israel, is yet sounded forth. Who is on the Lord's side in the great strife between good and evil, between religion and irreligion, between virtue and vice? There is a cause of God in the world now, as there was in the days of Moses.

As then the Almighty was, by the ministry of his prophet, leading his chosen people to the land of promise, and preparing them, by instruction and discipline, to receive and transmit to future ages his holy truth, so now is he, by the Gospel of his Son, Jesus Christ, leading the human race from the worse than Egyptian bondage of ignorance and vice, to the promised land of virtue, wisdom, and happiness, making ready for himself a peculiar people, zealous of good works. Wherever there is a question for moral judgment, wherever there is a right and wrong, wherever any thing can be done for the good of a fellow-being, or any thing avoided by which a fellow-being may be injured, wherever faith encourages, or conscience warns, or temptation assails us, there is the cause of God at issue, there is the demand addressed to us, "Who is on the Lord's side?" We are engaged in a warfare. Happier, indeed, than those of the tribe of Levi, who gathered at the call of Moses, the weapons of our warfare are not carnal; we wrestle not with flesh and blood; nor are we called to maintain the cause of God, as those in a ruder age, and under a less perfect dispensation, by deeds of sanguinary justice. No; our great ministry is love. Our leader is he who went about doing good, and our task, to follow his example. With us, as Christians, the service of God and the service of our race are one and the same; and he who is on the side of human rights and human happiness is on the Lord's side.

Are you on the Lord's side? Have you pledged yourself to his service? Are you doing all you can in his cause? When the Israelites heard from the lips of Moses that stern demand, they knew that the duty required of them was not silence, not neutrality, but a prompt acknowledgment of their allegiance to the Almighty, and a faithful performance of that which he, through his prophet, might command them. The summons was in the name, and by the authority, of their God. It was made by his chosen prophet, and in his holy cause. It was for them to choose between obedience and rebellion. How stands the case with us? Not Moses, but Christ, calls us to the service of the Lord; and that service is not one of vengeance, but of love. Yet is the call less imperative? Is it less our duty to be faithful Christians than it was that of the people in the days of Moses to be faithful Israelites? How, then, if they were guilty who refused to make profession of their faith at the voice of Moses, shall they be held guiltless who refuse the profession of their faith in Christ? It is by becoming members of the Christian Church that we take our stand, in the sight of God and man, on the side of Christian truth and Christian virtue, on the side of man's improvement and of God's commands.

INSTITUTION AND MEANING OF THE COMMUNION.

THE ordinance of the Lord's Supper derives its explanation from the circumstances under which it was instituted. Our Saviour, the night before he was crucified, was partaking with his disciples of the Passover, the feast appointed in commemoration of the great deliverance of the chosen people from the Egyptians. He availed himself of the occasion, — and a more suitable one could not have been chosen, — to institute another feast, commemorative of a greater deliverance. He took a portion of the bread which was before him, and, breaking it, compared it to his body, which was the next day to be broken on the cross. He then shared it among his disciples. He took a portion of the wine before him, and, pouring it forth, told his followers that thus his blood was to be poured forth. He passed the cup also around among them, and directed them to continue the custom in memory of him.

Such seems to be the plain account of the Christian communion. The bread and the wine are simply emblems of the Saviour's body and blood; and our participation in them is intended to remind us of what our Lord endured for our sake. Many Christians believe that there is a mysterious meaning, beyond this, implied in the words of Jesus, "This is my body," and "This is my blood." But nothing was more common with our Saviour than to employ figurative language. When he said, "I am the vine," "I am the door of the sheep," we readily understand that he only meant to compare himself to those objects; and it appears to us equally clear, that, when he said of the wine before him, "This is my blood," nothing more than a simple comparison was intended.

We are told respecting the three thousand who were converted on the day of Pentecost, soon after our Saviour's ascension, that "they continued steadfastly in the Apostles' doctrine and fellowship, and in *breaking of bread*, and in prayers." We are further told, that they continued "daily with one accord in the temple, and *breaking bread* from house to house." Acts ii. 42, 46. It seems from this, that, in the very earliest days of the Christian Church, whenever a number of the believers met together, they were accustomed to partake of bread and wine in memory of their Master. But if such was the custom, it was soon subjected to limitations. The first day of the week, the day hallowed by the resurrection and ascension of the Saviour, became the regular season for the religious meetings of his disciples; and it appears that on that day they were accustomed to assemble for the especial purpose of commemorating their Master in this ordinance. This we may collect from the passage in Acts xx. 7, — "And upon the first day of the week, when the disciples came together to break bread, Paul preached unto them."

We may reasonably suppose that, in the early churches generally, the religious design of this ordinance was kept in view, and the observance of it conducted in a reverential manner. In the luxurious city of Corinth, however, some abuses crept in, which drew from the Apostle Paul a severe rebuke.

Corinth was noted for wealth and dissoluteness; and it is evident from the tenor of St. Paul's first epistle to the church in that place, that the infection of the manners prevalent around them had found its way among the Christian community. The Corinthian disciples, when they came together on the Lord's day, were accustomed, like other Christians, to bring with them bread and wine for the rite commemorative of the Saviour. After the Apostle had left their city, the love of show and of indulgence prompted them, it appears, to contribute in this manner far more than was desirable for the emblematic purpose of the rite in which they were to engage. The simple feast of love was changed into a banquet. Probably the corruption was gradual; and for some time the festival, though too luxurious for propriety, was shared equally by all, and with reference in the minds of all to the circumstances under which it was instituted. But at length those circumstances seem to have been forgotten; the wealthy, who contributed largely to the banquet, rendered it in some instances an occasion of indecorous excess, while the poor were excluded from the table which they had not the means to assist in furnishing. This account of the celebration of the communion in a Christian church in the days of the Apostles may well surprise us; but it is too well attested to be called in question. The abuse, with others which existed in the same community, attracted the notice of St. Paul. He wrote to them in the following words: — "Now in this that I declare unto you, I praise you not, that ye come together, not for the better, but for the worse"; — that your religious meetings are not suited for your improvement, but for your corruption. "When ye come together therefore into one place, this is not to eat the Lord's Supper"; — this is not the proper way of observing such an ordinance. "For in eating, every one taketh before other his own supper: and one is hungry, and another is drunken. What! have ye not houses to eat and to drink in? or despise ye the church of God, and shame them that have not? What shall I say to you? Shall I praise you in this? I praise you not." He then reminds them of the meaning of the ordinance, of which it seems they had so generally lost sight. He adds: — "For as often as ye eat this bread, and drink this cup, ye do show the Lord's death till he come. Wherefore, whosoever shall eat this bread, and drink this cup of the Lord, unworthily, shall be guilty of the body and blood of the Lord. But let a man examine himself, and so let him eat of that bread, and drink of that cup. For he that eateth and drinketh unworthily, eateth and drinketh damnation to himself, not discerning the Lord's body." "Wherefore, my brethren, when ye come together to eat, tarry one for another. And if any man hunger, let him eat at home; that ye come not together unto condemnation." 1 Cor. xi. 17 – 34.

The language of the Apostle explains itself. The strong terms in which he speaks of eating and drinking unworthily, have probably deterred many from joining in the communion, who should have felt that it was both their duty and their right. But on examination, we perceive that St. Paul referred with disapprobation, not to the conduct of any who reverently, and with a desire to honor their Master, comply with his command, but to an abuse which has not perhaps existed in the Church from the days of the Corinthians to the present time; a total perversion of the ordinance, in forgetfulness of its meaning, to the purpose of mere sensual indulgence. This the Apostle rightly called "not discerning the Lord's body," — not distinguishing between the emblems of the Lord's body and the food used in common banquets; and this was surely partaking unworthily. That this crime might be avoided, he bade the Corinthians to examine themselves, that they might know with what views and feelings they approached the table of the Lord.

This passage, therefore, does not exclude from Christian communion any one who reverences the

Saviour, and understands that the Supper is administered in commemoration of him. The Apostle, however, in the same letter, gives directions to the Corinthian church to suspend from their fellowship a man who had committed a flagrant offence. 1 Cor. v. The order was obeyed, and the individual repented. The second epistle requests the church to forgive, and again receive the penitent among them. 2 Cor. ii. 5 – 10.

HISTORICAL IMPORTANCE OF THE COMMUNION.

THE Lord's Supper is an historical memorial of important transactions, — a perpetual witness to the truth of the Christian religion. That we may judge of its value in this respect, we must take a brief view of the nature of such memorials.

Monuments and commemorations of past events have been in use among almost every people. These have mostly taken the form either of some remarkable structure, as a heap of stones, an altar, or a column; or of some national observance, as a feast, or a pilgrimage.

The monumental structure bears witness through succeeding ages to the occasion on which it was erected, even if no inscription be engraved upon it; because they who witnessed its erection hand down the memory of that event, and the transactions connected with it, to their children, and they to theirs, and these to still following generations. True, the traditional account may by time be blended with error; but this is most likely to be the case in monuments of merely local interest. If we find substantially the same account given of any monument, the work of human hands, by the widely scattered descendants of those who witnessed its erection, we have strong reason to believe that this account is true.

A heap of stones, an altar, or a pillar, may crumble to decay. But the record engraven on the customs of a people cannot be destroyed, except by the destruction of the nation itself. As an instance of such a record, we may select our own observance of our national anniversary. Let it be supposed that our nation should relapse into the deepest barbarism, — arts, letters, sciences, being extinguished, but our observance of the national anniversary still continuing. In that case, a thousand years hence, that anniversary would still furnish the information of our revolutionary struggle. The people would always necessarily connect with it the tradition of the Declaration of Independence, and of the war during which it was made. If at any time an attempt should be made to trace the observance of the Fourth of July to some other origin, the people would answer, ignorant as they might be in other respects, — "The account you give of our national feast is new to us; it cannot, therefore, be true. The account we give is that which has been handed down alike in all parts of our country, and has, therefore, evidently been the same through all ages since its origin. It therefore must be true."

We return now to the ordinance of the Lord's Supper. The whole Christian world unite in receiving that ordinance as an institution of the Saviour, in which he distinctly foretold his own approaching death. In thousands of churches, throughout the world, among Oriental Christians, Catholics, and Protestants, the bread and wine are distributed, and accompanied with the words, "This is my body," "This is my blood," and "This do in remembrance of me." Ask the Christian of America, of Russia, or of Spain, to say by whom this rite was established; and each will answer, By Jesus Christ. Nor does he gain his knowledge of this fact from books. It is from tradition. We all see the rite administered, or the preparations made for it in our churches, and receive a general idea of its purpose and origin before we are old enough to read intelligently the accounts in the Gospels. The ordinance has always been thus administered. This is the account which we all have received from our fathers, and they from theirs; and it must, therefore, be true.

Could we, if we had never before heard of the Lord's Supper, or seen it administered, be induced by any assurances to believe that we had known and participated in such an ordinance, and had been familiar with it from our childhood? And is it more probable that our ancestors, two or ten generations since, were thus deceived? — that they could be made to believe that an altar which was raised in their very sight was a time-honored memorial-altar which they had known from infancy? At what time was this mighty fraud effected? History answers not. There is no trace in her records of any period, since the time of Christ, when an attempt was made to introduce, or to revive, the observance of the Supper. That observance, therefore, we conclude, has been held continually in the Christian Church, from the days of its Divine founder.

But could such an institution have been fraudulently introduced at a period soon after the death of the Saviour? Could the Christian community, ten or twenty years after that event, have been persuaded that their Master in a solemn manner instituted this rite, if they had never heard of it before? Or, to go back the single step that remains, could one of the Apostles have persuaded the rest that their Master had, in the presence of them all, established such an ordinance, when they had no remembrance of such a scene? If not, the conclusion irresistibly follows, that the communion was instituted by Jesus of Nazareth the night before his death.

Let us now approach and read the inscription on this venerable altar; — in other words, let us notice the language in which the Saviour established this ordinance. "Take, eat; this is my body, which is broken for you: this do in remembrance of me." "This cup is the new testament [or covenant] in my blood: this do ye, as oft as ye drink it, in remembrance of me." 1 Cor. xi. 24, 25. These words, in substance, are inseparable from the ordinance. It would be nothing without them. We know, therefore, that these words were uttered by Jesus before he was put to death. What does this prove?

It proves that Jesus, while banqueting with his disciples, foretold his own violent death, and with so much certainty of the fulfilment of his prophecy, that he instituted an ordinance in memory of the event.

It proves that his prophecy was fulfilled, and that he was violently put to death. Otherwise, the observance of the rite among his followers would have been but mockery.

It proves that his death was voluntary; for it shows that he knew his danger, and that, instead of taking measures to escape or to resist, he remained where it was certain to come upon him, foretold the result, and even rendered it necessary to his own cause; for he would have been proved a false prophet, if his enemies had not succeeded in their design against his life.

It proves that he acted from benevolent motives, and those of the most elevated kind; for no others could be found to induce a man voluntarily to submit to a tormenting, and, as it was then regarded, a shameful death.

It proves, then, that he spoke what he believed to be the truth. Can we conceive of a man, whose whole life is one continued falsehood, becoming a voluntary martyr to the noblest principles of benevolence?

It proves, then, that his religion is true; for that religion presents claims respecting the truth of which he could not have been mistaken.

Thus have we reached this great conclusion, the truth of the Christian religion, plainly deducible from the existence throughout the world, at this day, of the ordinance of the Lord's Supper.

If all the records of our faith were swept away, and there remained, besides this rite, only some traditions respecting the history of our Saviour's life and death, the argument we have now contemplated would not be overthrown. It does not depend on the authenticity of writings. It stands in its own strength, an immovable pillar, though comparatively an unnoticed one, among the thousand which support the temple of Gospel truth.

FOR WHOM IS THE COMMUNION INTENDED?

A QUESTION of great practical importance presents itself. For whom is the communion intended? Some limitations are given by general consent, and by the nature of the ordinance itself. No one, probably, in this age, would be disposed to admit to the Lord's table, children whose early age prevents them from understanding the meaning of the emblems exhibited, or persons whose immoral lives would be a scandal to the Church of Christ. The exclusion of the latter class is, indeed, sanctioned by the example of the Corinthian church, under the direction of St. Paul. 1 Cor. v.; 2 Cor. ii. 6 – 10; vii. 11. The ordinance of baptism, also, being the proper form of introduction to the Church, should be received before the disciple partakes of the communion. Belief in Christ, and a determination to live according to his law, appear the only other requisites which we are authorized to demand.

It may be asked, however, if those who desire to unite in this ordinance should not possess the evidence within themselves that they have experienced that change of heart which our Saviour describes as regeneration ?

If by regeneration is meant the commencement of a pious life, by the serious direction of the thoughts towards religion, — in other words, the recognition of the truth, that we are bound in duty to serve our God, and the adoption of this truth as the ground of conduct for the future, — then, certainly, we say that no one, unless thus regenerate, should approach the table of the Lord. It would be mockery for one to draw nigh thither, who had as yet no serious purpose to obey the religion of Him whom he thus in outward form acknowledges as his Master. But if the inquiry relates rather to the inward working of the Holy Spirit than to its result in the determination of the will, — if it be questioned whether one can lawfully partake of the communion, until he is conscious of feelings such as can only be accounted for by the direct agency of the spirit of God, — then would we reply, that the condition thus suggested is unreasonable. The voice of God's spirit to the heart comes, we have reason to believe, in a manner not always distinguishable from the general current of the thoughts and feelings. While some are able to state with considerable accuracy the period of their conversion, others — and among them many eminent for piety in various denominations — are unable to remember the time when they began to love and honor their Maker. "Secret things belong to God"; and among such mysteries we may well class the nature and boundaries of that intercourse which he maintains, by his Holy Spirit, with our souls. To us belongs the plain duty of obeying our Saviour's plain commands.

Nor is it in our power to fix on any particular degree of moral attainment which shall qualify the disciple for attendance on the Supper of his Lord. The most virtuous man, the sincerest Christian, must not bring to that hallowed ordinance the feeling that he is without sin; the true penitent may humbly approach, though the past offences which he has now for ever renounced with detestation, should be "as scarlet." This, indeed, may justly be required, that none should, by this ordinance, make profession of his faith in Christ, who, either by inveterate and unconquered evil habits, or by notorious fickleness of disposition, is likely to bring discredit on the cause of religion.

Should any one, for instance, in a former irreligious life, have been guilty of habitual profanity, let him not feel that regret for such a sin, however sincere, authorizes him at once to connect himself with the Church of Christ. Let him rather first prove his strength to overcome the old evil habit; and when this has been successfully tested by time, he may join his fellow-disciples at the table of the Lord, without incurring the danger of "giving occasion to the enemy to blaspheme."

For whom, then, is the communion intended?

It is intended for the humble believer; for him who, having examined as far as he had the power, rests in the conviction that the Gospel of Christ is true. Yes, though occasionally doubts may pass across his mind, — though he may be at times in the spirit of him who said, "Lord, I believe; help thou mine unbelief"; yet if his faith, though trembling, rests on the sure ground of deliberate, impartial examination, — if he feels that he has good reason for believing, — the communion is intended for him. It will give strength to his wavering confidence. It will reassure his doubting spirit. He will be brought by it into the presence of Jesus, and hear his words; and doubt and fear will vanish as he listens.

The communion is intended for the young disciple, — young in Christian experience, whether he be of many or of few years, — who has entered sufficiently upon the course of piety to be firm in his own determination to pursue it, but who feels still that he has much to learn, that he has difficulties to encounter, and trials to overcome. Let him not be discouraged. Let him not think that it would be presumption in him to approach the table of the Lord. If he has reason to be persuaded that, by the grace of God, his union with the visible Church will not be dishonored by his desertion of the path he has chosen, let him not be dismayed because he knows that the path has its difficulties. Let him delay as long as prudence requires, but let him not permanently dispense with the invaluable aid in a Christian course which a participation in the communion will impart. That will render religion more a personal thing to him than it otherwise could be. It will give him a deeper interest in the individual character and sufferings of Jesus Christ. It will present stated seasons for religious reflection and the examination of himself. Let him not, by unfounded fears, deprive himself of these advantages.

The communion is intended for the parent. It will introduce religion into the bosom of his family. It will set before his children the blessed example of their father's reverence for religion ; an example speaking louder than a thousand precepts. It is intended for the afflicted. It will bring before the eye of faith the picture of the Saviour's patient endurance, and of his love, stronger than death itself. It is intended for the happy. It will lead their minds up from the enjoyment of God's gifts to the knowledge and love of their bestower. It will warm their hearts towards their heavenly friend, their Redeemer, and cause their feelings of joy to be expanded and purified into a sympathy with all happiness, and a fervent desire to diminish all misery, throughout the world which that Redeemer came to bless.

REASONS FOR ATTENDING THE COMMUNION.

Our Lord Jesus Christ still spreads his table, still invites us to the simple feast by which he is commemorated. But, as in the parable which he himself related, of a certain king who made a great supper, how many of those to whom the invitation comes, begin with one consent to make excuse! Some refrain because the rite is in their apprehension without meaning; others, because they are well aware that it means too much for them to unite in it, — that it implies a promise of consistent service to God and to Christ, which they are not yet resolved to render. One declines because the standard of conduct among professing Christians is too low; another, because the standard of conduct in the law of Christ is too high, — too high for his own worldly inclinations and principles.

Let us take a view of the considerations which should lead the believer in Christ to unite in the observance of the Lord's Supper.

In the first place, if there were no perceptible advantage arising either to ourselves or others from attendance on the ordinance of Christian communion, and apart also from all considerations of devotional or affectionate feeling, it is our duty, because it is commanded by him who speaks to us in the name of God. "This do," said our Saviour, "in remembrance of me." The voice of love in which he spoke, the motive of love which he presented, should not make those who reverence him forget that he is authorized to command them. "This," said the holy voice on the Mount of Transfiguration, "is my beloved Son; hear ye him." Shall we not, then, obey the call of him who comes to us thus, the commissioned messenger of his Heavenly Father? It may be that the purposes of the ordinance are to us obscure; but if they were altogether unknown, would it not be enough that we are commanded to observe it? Is a child to know the purpose of every direction his parent gives, before he determines whether he will obey it? Let it be enough for us, though there were naught else to engage us, that our Saviour hath required it, — he who was authorized to speak in the name of his Father and our Father, of his God and our God.

Yet is there a doubt on our minds, whether those words of his were truly a command, or whether that command, if given, is applicable to us? Let us contemplate the example of our Lord himself under circumstances which authorized a similar doubt. John was baptizing in Judea. There was no provision of God's written law, requiring that all should receive this baptism. The prophet invited all, and many of the devout received the rite at his hands. Among those who offered themselves to his ministration was one, so pure, so holy in character, that John himself felt that the penitential rite could not have to him its full application. He hesitated. "I have need to be baptized of thee," said he, "and comest thou to me?" But Jesus replied, "Suffer it to be so now, for thus it becometh us to fulfil all righteousness." He would not plead exemption from a common duty. He would not make curious questions with regard to the imperative character of the calls of religion. Let the meek obedience of our Saviour be a lesson to us.

In the next place, apart from the consideration of duty in obeying an express command, we owe to Christ himself this expression of our reverence and love to him. For our sakes, — among millions of others, indeed, yet truly for our sakes, — did the Redeëmer give in his life the holiest lessons, both in word and conduct, and finally lay down that life upon the cross. We believe that he did so. He asks of us to express that belief in a peculiar, and very easy and simple manner. We surely owe it to him to comply with this request. If it be said that now, removed from this world, our Saviour can have no knowledge of what we do, and derive no pleasure from it, it may be answered, in the first place, that this assertion takes for granted what admits of discussion. We are not authorized to assert that the blessed Jesus is not still conversant with the actions and the feelings of those whom he came to save. In the second place, our obligation to cherish the memory of a friend depends not on his knowledge whether we fulfil it. It would be ungrateful in a child to forget his parent, — in a nation to lose the memory of the hero who had wrought its deliverance, — though the parent and the hero were resting in the grave. Gratitude, then, to our holy Saviour, calls upon us to remember him in the way he pointed out, and thus to acknowledge his name in the presence of our fellow-men.

This obligation of gratitude appears stronger

when we remember that this rite is not an unmeaning form, but wisely appointed by Christ as a means of reminding us of the most impressive, most affecting portion of his history. In the last peaceful hour he enjoyed before his tortures, he chose one simple emblem to represent his body that was to be lacerated and broken, another to remind us of his blood that was to be shed. If, then, we have a feeling of gratitude to him, we shall desire to keep alive and strengthen that feeling; and, apart from the fact of his having appointed it, there could be nothing more suitable in itself for that purpose than a custom which thus brings before us the remembrance of his voluntary sufferings for the sake of mankind.

Not only is our attendance on the communion due from us to our Master personally; it is due to the religion of which he is the head, — to the holy cause for which he gave his life. That cause is the cause of God and of man; and the ordinance in question is that by which we express towards it our allegiance. It is the cause of God; for Christ made known to the world the true character of the Creator, revealing him to us as a God of love and of holiness. In proportion as the Christian religion is received and appreciated in the world, will the Divine Being be truly and worthily known and honored. That for which Christ died is the cause of man, for our best hopes for man's improvement and happiness must be connected with the spread of the Gospel. It is this which must put an end to war, by teaching the lesson of love; to slavery, by teaching justice; to intemperance, by teaching self-restraint. It is this, this alone, faith in God as Christ has revealed him to us, which can conquer every evil passion of our race, subdue selfishness, and render mankind a band of brothers, aiding each other in their path to the highest good of which their present existence is capable. And, far more, it is this which alone can prepare man for heaven, can remove from before the sight of the mourner the cloud that darkens the grave, and bid the rays of heavenly light shine through. It is this, if any thing, which must make man feel that he is an immortal being, and act in a manner to prepare himself for the fulness of his immortality. It is, then, the cause of God and man that claims the profession of our allegiance. And can it be doubted that the rite in question is the mode of expressing that profession? Baptism, as administered among us, cannot be so regarded. Attendance at worship is practised alike by those who are deeply interested in religion, and those who are not. Those, then, who desire to see the Redeemer's cause prospering in the world, are bound to express their own allegiance to it, in the way generally recognized among Christians, and appointed by the Master himself. Our duty here resembles that which every citizen owes to what he deems correct principles in public affairs; to give his vote for them. By professing Christianity we give to it our vote; we throw our personal influence into the scale of the Gospel.

Not only do we owe this duty to the world, or more distinctly to the community in which we reside; we owe it to our own familiar friends, our own domestic circles. By a profession of religion, we give a distinct and public testimony to its worth, adding weight to all other testimony we may bear in its favor. A young man may advise his companions to a virtuous and pious course, and it is well; but it will probably have still more effect on them, if, in addition to his advice, he distinctly pledges *himself* to the course he recommends. A father may teach his children to love God, and honor their Saviour's commands, and it is well; but it will be better still, if, together with this, he shows them by a public profession that he himself desires to do as he instructs them to do. At the Passover, that solemn feast on which the communion was founded, it was customary among the Jews, that, when they had assembled around the board, one of the children should inquire, What mean ye by this service? At this prepared suggestion, one of the older persons told the tale of that great deliverance to commemorate which the Passover had been instituted; and the young learned reverence and gratitude from perceiving these sentiments expressed by their parents.

Again, we are called on to participate in this ordinance, by our regard for the purity and life of the Christian Church itself. There are many who complain that the Church is not doing, for the good of mankind and the glory of God, all that it ought to do. No doubt the complaint is well founded. It is in accordance with the testimony of Scripture, as to the weakness of human purposes, and with the witness borne by the consciences of Christians to their own deficiencies. But the professed followers of Christ may well reply to those who thus complain, Friends, will you not aid us more by joining us, and adding your strength to ours, than by merely reproaching us with that imperfection which we are ready to acknowledge? The work which our Master, Christ, has left us, the work of making his religion triumphant in the world, of doing good unto all men, and keeping ourselves pure from evil, is enough to engage all our best powers, and deserves the combined effort of all who in their hearts honor their Redeemer.

In no age of the world, perhaps, has the great purpose of the Church of Christ been more clearly, more gloriously, presented before it than it is now. This is a period of agitation, an age of revolutions. There are mighty elements at work to effect changes, mighty powers engaged to resist those changes. Amid the storm, it is only the voice of Christian love that can say, Peace, be still! Let the Church awake to her duty. Let those of ardent mind, who now denounce her, bring their ardor to her service, and suffer her gentleness to blend therewith. Let her calm, majestic voice be heard, bearing testimony against every form of evil, and her hand uplift before the eager combatants the cross, emblem of meekness, patience, truth, and love, with its inscription as in the legendary vision of old time, — "In this overcome."

Attendance on this commemorative ordinance is also a part of the duty which the Christian owes to himself. Beset with temptations as we are, with the world offering to us continual inducements to neglect the cultivation of our higher nature, we need every holy influence of which we can avail ourselves. If we perceive not this need, that very unconsciousness shows the urgency of our necessity. But who, that is sincerely and manfully striving to make his own character what God approves, does not feel that he needs all the aid which religion can afford him? Among the means of spiritual improvement, the communion holds a place on two distinct grounds, — as a mark of Christian profession, and from the emotions which in itself it is suited to excite. As a mark of Christian profession, it is a pledge to God and man of the intention of those who assume it to live worthily of the name by which they are called; and the expression of a virtuous resolution is always regarded as one means of gaining strength for its fulfilment. It has been recommended by religious writers, that the Christian should draw up a solemn act of self-dedication to the service of his God, and, with due deliberation and prayer, affix to it his signature. In the observance of the communion, however, such an act is implied. None can for the first time assume a place among those who profess the name of Christ, without feeling that a solemn pledge has been given, which God has witnessed no less than man, and which henceforth it must be the effort of life to maintain.

And, by the feelings which in itself it excites, the communion has an influence too valuable for the disciple to dispense with. At this table we meet our Saviour. We *commune* with him. We have our great model placed, more distinctly than at other times, before our view. Sympathy is excited for his sufferings, love for his self-devotion, emulation of his stainless virtue, and the desire to share, in some degree, his harmony of spirit with the Supreme. In the solemn stillness with which the exercises are varied, the soul turns its glance inward, and self-examination points out what duty has yet to accomplish, while the ardent vow to fulfil the task appointed is rendered more holy by the prayer that Heaven will give us strength for its performance.

Lastly, to the thoughtful Christian, should not this hallowed act be the natural result of the feelings within? If we love and reverence Christ, why fear to profess it? If we desire to do right, why not avow, and thus strengthen, that desire? It is a part of the experience of a religious character, essential to the completeness of the whole; and if the character be truly and thoroughly Christian, it should seem that self-denial, if exerted at all, must be used to keep us from the hallowed table, not to overcome our reluctance to approach it.

Come, then, with us, may the disciple say to those who hesitate, and we will do you good. Nay, rather, come with us, and our Master, Christ, and his holy Gospel and its ordinances, and the God from whom they came, will bless us all, and enable us to aid and to bless each other.

LORD! I AM NOT WORTHY.—Matt. VIII. 8.

No grace is more lovely than true Christian humility; no grace, perhaps, more difficult to attain, and to preserve in its due strength, alike without diminution and without alloy. The very consciousness that we possess it is dangerous to its existence. Yet it is indispensable. Scarce any quality is sooner missed by the observant eye of the world; for pride and vanity are faults that lie on the surface, obvious to the sight of all; and though in their smaller degrees they may be classed among venial sins, yet, when they have attained their full power, they are equally despicable in the sight of men, and offensive in that of God.

True humility results from a right appreciation of our own relation to the Supreme Being and to our fellow-creatures. We are to feel, as we look upward, that we are children of a day in the presence of the Eternal, — imperfect and sinful in the presence of the All-Pure. We are to feel, as we look round on our fellow-men, that we are of them, not above them; that our natures are like theirs, our powers of mind and body similar, our destiny for eternity the same. Over each of our brethren the Universal Father watches, as over us. To each he has promised the same heaven as to us, and on the same conditions. We know that there is nothing which we possess, either internal or external, which we have not received from the Divine Giver. We are to feel, therefore, that there is nothing of which we can glory, as if it were in truth our own. But perhaps the feeling of humility results not so much from any other view, as from that in which we contemplate ourselves as sinful, recall to memory our many transgressions of the Divine law, and bring our own imperfection into immediate contrast with the high standard of duty as set forth in word and deed by our Saviour. Then, indeed, does it appear to us that boasting is excluded; then, indeed, as we listen to the Saviour's invitations of love, the Father's promises of mercy, are we ready to exclaim, Lord! I am not worthy.

We are not worthy that the Saviour should come to us; — the world, when he came, was not worthy that he should abide in a fleshly tabernacle and mingle among its blinded and defiled spirits. Nor are we, at this day, worthy of the grace that is granted to us, in the Saviour's coming to us through his word and through his ordinances. If worthiness be taken in its strict, primitive sense, these mercies of God have been, and are yet, conferred on the undeserving; but in that sense which mercy recognizes, we are worthy, — we are worthy of assistance, for we need assistance. Our plea is not our merit, but our necessity.

Humility is true and proper, when, proceeding from thoughts like these, it suggests to us the inadequacy of our efforts, if unassisted by the grace of God. It should teach us to depend, not on ourselves alone, but on his aid, freely and kindly given to our sincere efforts. True humility will be far from rendering us hopeless or discouraged. It points us to the never-failing Source of strength. It leads us to the Rock that is higher than we; and, while it deprives our works of obedience of the pretence to perfection in themselves, it gives to them new dignity and value, as those offerings of faith and love on which the Eternal King has deigned to smile.

But there is a false as well as a true humility. This heavenly grace is not, more than any other, exempted from the danger attending human virtue, in this world of trial, — the danger of running into extremes, and changing its real character for one far less acceptable to God and profitable to man.

Perhaps the plea of mistaken humility is never so frequently brought forward, as for the neglect of attendance upon the table of the Lord. It is, in fact, the general plea. "I am not worthy to become a member of the Christian Church," is the language, and, no doubt, the sincere language, of thousands. "I am conscious of so many frailties, of being so far from the character which God requires, that I feel that it would be presumption in me to class myself among the professed disciples of the Redeemer." That there are those by whom this language might be used with propriety, we are far from denying. We have no wish to see persons who are really unworthy, and whose conduct would do dishonor to the Christian name, pressing to the table of the Lord. But the objection is less frequently urged by such than by a different class, — the class of those who are trying to do right, — who respect religion, and whose lives are influenced by its teachings, — the very class who most need the hallowed influence of the communion, to give strength to their faith and vigor to their purposes, and for the consistency of whose profession none but themselves would entertain any apprehension.

Christian friend, distrust in yourself that humility which would keep you from the discharge of plain and positive duty. If, indeed, your character has been, and continues to be, such as will render your assumption of a Christian profession disgraceful to the Church, and thereby injurious to others, you have previous duties to discharge, — those of repentance and reformation. If you be engaged in those great tasks, continue them, until you feel a reasonable assurance that your conduct will give no occasion to the adversaries of religion to speak reproachfully, but wait not for an unattainable perfection before you discharge the duty to which your Saviour has called you. And in reference both to this subject and to every other, let true humility ever be the companion of your way. Conscious of your own weakness, look continually to God for strength to aid your efforts; conscious of your own sins, strive ever to conquer them, and to advance, day by day, nearer to the heavenly mark, the prize of Christian excellence. Humility should lead you, not to despond, but to be watchful in effort, and constant in prayer. If temptation is conquered, ascribe the glory to the

Lord, whose aid was with you. If temptation is, in an evil hour, allowed to conquer, remember, while you mourn over your fall, that the mercies of the Lord are from everlasting to everlasting, that true repentance is always acceptable in his sight, and that for the strength which you have lost through sin, it becomes you to walk with the more circumspection, and to look to him with more of beseeching earnestness. But despond not. Shrink not from your duties. Abuse not the name of humility, to make it an excuse for neglect. If your heart breathes forth, "Lord, I am not worthy that thou shouldst come under my roof," strive to become more deserving, and meantime let your petition be, "Lord, come in thine own worthiness, and not in mine."

WHAT IS THAT TO THEE? FOLLOW THOU ME. — JOHN XXI. 22.

HUMAN beings are, by the constitution of their natures, liable to be influenced by each other. Sometimes the principle of imitation, sometimes the opposite propensity to be unlike others, controls our course of conduct. Within certain bounds, this is right. The propensity to imitation, especially, is of high value in the early, the forming period of our lives. But it must be remembered, still, that there is a relation between every human being and his Maker, in which no third person bears a part; — that the man is answerable for himself, and is guilty or not guilty, according as he acts in conformity to his own conscience or against it. The wrong that we do is not less truly evil, because we may have followed a multitude to do it. The good that we have omitted to do was not less truly our duty, because others neglected to do it, or discharged it in an imperfect or erroneous manner. Independence in our actions is often no less required of us by religion, than it is by true manliness of character. Without it, we forfeit consistency and self-approval. The things that we would, we do not, and those that we would not, those we do. The mind, meantime, is neither satisfied with itself, nor certain what course it should pursue. It is inquiring what others do, instead of asking of the law of God what is its own duty. And, as the conduct of others is infinitely various, it is embarrassed and divided among conflicting courses, when a plain, straightforward path lies open before it, in which it would go on, without doubt or fear, if but once fully decided to follow Christ and duty.

Let us, if we feel disposed to hesitate from regard to the conduct or the opinion of others, where our own duty is clear, remember the words of Jesus to his Apostle, "What is that to thee? Follow thou me." Let us not be withheld by fear, or by any other cause, connected with the imperfect and erring beings around us, from doing what we feel to be right. An independent course is by no means inconsistent with due respect to the judgment of others. We may be ignorant, and others may be wise, we may be sinful, and they may be eminently virtuous, yet, in regard to our own duty, we must walk by our own light, not by theirs. We may seek from them advice or information, we may sit in all humility at their feet, to learn their wisdom and behold their virtues, but when an occasion arises for us to act, if they or the whole world point to one course, and conscience and God's word to the opposite, conscience and God's word must be obeyed.

What are the most common excuses made for the neglect of the communion? Few question the fact that the Saviour of mankind left to his disciples an ordinance which gratitude and duty alike require them to observe. Yet thousands who believe in the truth of Christ's religion, and who are not without a sense of gratitude to the God and the Saviour from whom it came, turn away from the fulfilment of this obligation. What are the reasons which they assign? Some, undoubtedly, can plead motives of a conscientious character, which, whether altogether derived from correct views or not, are yet entitled to respect. Let us examine some of the reasons assigned by others.

"I," replies one, "would willingly obey the last

command of the Saviour, were it not that I should stand nearly alone in so doing, among the circle with which I am connected. My conduct, were I to join the Church, would have the aspect of singularity, perhaps of presumption. Why others, older and wiser than myself, hold back, I cannot understand; but while they do, it is not for me to press forward." To the person urging such an objection as this, we may reply, The service you are called on to render is an individual one, and for which you are individually responsible. Those whose example you follow in abstaining are acting for themselves, and are responsible to that God who alone sees their hearts. But to you, independent of them, the command of the Saviour comes, "Follow thou me"; and there rests on you, independently of others, the responsibleness of determining whether you will obey it. If others do, as it appears to you, wrong, you may grieve for their error, though it were better still to suspend, if possible, your judgment, leaving it to Him who is their judge as well as yours; but as concerns the bearing of their conduct on yours, the word of the Saviour is, "What is that to thee? Follow thou me."

"For me," replies another, and the class is large, "I would join the Church of Christ, if I saw those who are its members conducting themselves worthily of their profession. But I cannot perceive that they are any more shining examples of virtue than other men. In fact, I have seen such violations of the law of Christ, so much of cant, formality, and hypocrisy, so much worldliness of spirit with a pretence of religion, in those who are called church-members, that I have no idea of becoming one of their number." Such language is not unfrequently used; it is easy to reply to it, that no one supposes that the fact of a man's joining the Church exempts him from the temptations common to human nature, and that the standard of character in the Church, though not as high as we could wish, is much higher than that in the community at large. But the reply already given, in the words of Christ, and made to the objector in his name, is amply sufficient to meet the case. "What is that to thee? Follow thou me." Let all the real deficiencies of the Church and church-members be admitted, they affect neither the command of the Lord, nor the duty of those who believe in him. If others have sinned, the evil they have done will be yet greater, if it have the effect of causing thee to neglect thy duty. If the cross of Christ has been borne by so many unfaithfully, still greater is the reason for increasing the scanty number of its faithful supporters. Assume it, then, thyself, neither despondingly nor proudly, — neither feeling that it will be dishonored in thy hands, nor claiming that thou canst bear it better than others have done; but calmly determined to do thine own duty to the best of thine ability, beseeching Divine assistance, and leaving the judgment of thyself and of others with God, to whom it belongs. If others have sinned, their sins are upon themselves; if they have done well, they will not fail of their reward; but what is that to thee, to affect thy conduct? Follow thou thy Saviour.

IS IT MY DUTY TO PARTAKE OF THE COMMUNION?

I AM called on to determine whether I will offer myself for reception to the Church. Let me view the important question in the light of duty, giving to every consideration, on either side, its due weight, but nothing more. I trust that I sincerely desire to do right. I would lay aside all unworthy thoughts, whether of ostentation in making a profession, or of timidity in declining it. It is a question of duty, and, viewing it in that solemn character, all such feelings as these must be relinquished. Ostentation! How can I think of such a thing in the presence of my God? Timidity! If, indeed, God calls me, shall I fear the face of man?

But does God indeed call me to an act of this kind? What is there in my circumstances that renders it more proper for me than for many others, who yet, I see, retire with me when the communion-table is spread? Some of them are my superiors in age and in character. While they withdraw, can I with propriety remain? Yet let me reflect. I know not their motives in withholding their attendance. I know not how far they are justified. I cannot judge them; God is their only judge; but is he not also mine? If others must decide for themselves in this matter what is right, must not I also for myself? Let me act, then, not according to what others deem their duty, but by what appears to me to be my own.

And if I find that I have been influenced by their example, let me reflect if others may not be by mine. Are none now prevented from uniting with the Church by seeing that I do not? At least, are none discouraged by seeing that crowd retire, of which I form one? Might not some be induced to think of their duty in this respect, if they knew that I had joined the Church? Cannot I think of some among my friends upon whom such an act on my part would have a useful influence?

By uniting with the Church, I should give my testimony in behalf of religion. Would not that testimony have its weight in commending religion to those I love?

But am I, indeed, fit to join the Church. My character is imperfect. I am often conscious of not exercising due self-restraint. Let me reflect upon my faults. What are my most easily besetting sins ?

As memory presents them to me, I shrink, indeed, from coming, thus weak and imperfect, to join the company of Christ's professed disciples. Yet let me reflect. Is it not as sinners that we must approach, if we would find acceptance ? Yes, but as *repentant* sinners. Am I, then, truly repentant ?

Is there a cherished sin, that I am unwilling to forsake ? If so, let me not venture to make a profession, which under such circumstances would be hypocritical. But so it must not be. Shall I prefer sin to holiness, destruction to salvation ?

I hope, I trust, that I am truly penitent. But I am conscious of weakness. As I have fallen into sin, so I may fall again ; and then, if I am a member of the Church, my offence will be more disgraceful to myself, and more injurious, than at present.

But are not all human beings liable to fall ? Shall none, then, join the Church, lest they should disgrace their profession ?

The question resolves itself to this. Is there a

reasonable probability that my future course will be such as shall not inflict dishonor on the cause of Christ?

I feel my own weakness, but is not my strength on high? God will sustain me, if I pray to him. Have I formed the habit of secret prayer? Is prayer with me an outward form merely, or is my heart there? Am I firm in my resolution to continue steadfast in prayer and effort?

Lord! thou knowest my weakness, be thou my strength!

Perhaps I can judge something of the permanence of my good resolutions by their past history. Are religious thoughts of recent date with me, excited by some sudden cause, or have they been for a length of time gradually developed? In the latter case, I may have more confidence that they will be permanent, than in the former.

Yet, in the former case, I must not quench the spirit. If it should appear, on full reflection, that I am not yet fitted to join the Church, let me at least resolve on such a course of life as shall give maturity to my present religious impressions. Daily prayer, reading of the Scriptures, self-examination from time to time, — say at some stated hour of every Sabbath, — let me resolve on these, as means for deepening and strengthening my religious character.

And should not the same course be pursued if I unite with the Church? Assuredly. Thus much, then, is at least attained. Lord! grant thy blessing, that I may keep the resolution.

I talk of joining the Church. But are not all believers really members of the Church of Christ? What right have the few who commune to arrogate that title to themselves alone?

Nay, but is it not rather true that others voluntarily relinquish that title, than that they assume it? If all are members of the Church, then should all partake of the Church's ordinances. And with us, all are at liberty to do this who believe in Christ, and are not excluded on account of immoral conduct. The distinction, then, between Church and congregation, so far as there is any thing wrong in it, is chargeable, not on those who commune, but on those who decline communing. If all did their duty, Church and congregation would be the same.

But are my feelings such, with regard to the communion, that I can with profit partake of it? Can it be edifying to me?

Can it be otherwise to contemplate my Saviour at the period of his course when his holy character was most touchingly displayed? Bread and wine are, indeed, but outward elements; but they are emblems of the Lord's body and blood. Am I so sensual that I cannot, in receiving them, think of their emblematic meaning?

I have said that I would at stated seasons examine myself. Will not the communion present the most suitable occasion for this duty? Let it be the task of every Lord's day; but sometimes I should comprehend in my survey a longer period of time than from one Sabbath to another; and when can this be more suitably done than at the communion?

Will it not aid me to keep my good resolutions, that I have thus professed them before my fellow-men and before my God?

Christ, my Saviour, requests this mark of gratitude from me. Can I refuse it?

Christ, my Master, commands this service. Shall I disobey?

I feel the force of considerations such as these. My only doubt must be, whether my conduct will be answerable to the profession I make. And this doubt, I know, ought not entirely to withhold me. It may require me to delay the act, until I have by experience tested my ability to walk according to the law of God. Yet let me remember that delay is dangerous. If I postpone at all this duty, let it be for a designated time; and let that time be given, as far as possible, to the careful use of the various means of Christian advancement. Have I not cause to fear even such delay, lest I lose something of my present interest? Aid me, O God, by the spirit of wisdom, that I may decide aright!

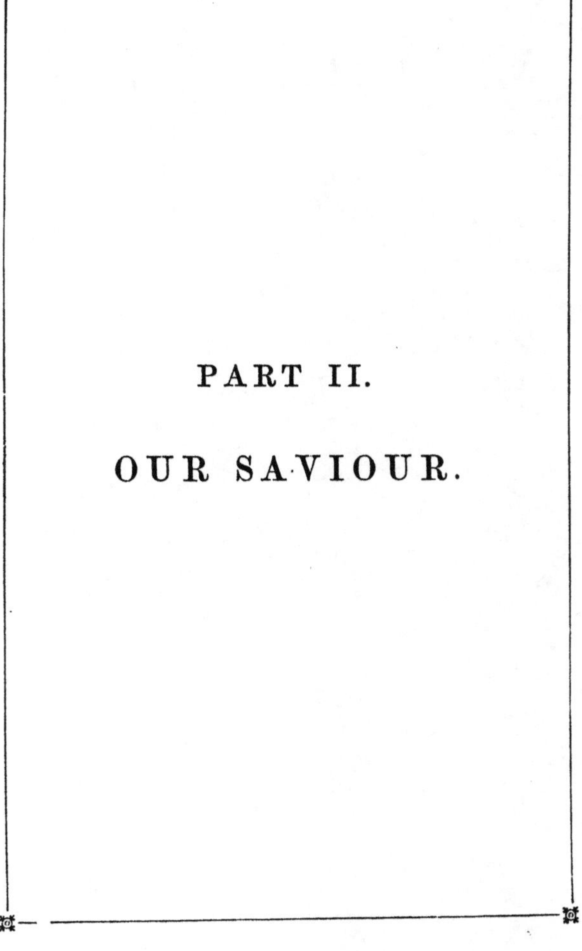

PART II.

OUR SAVIOUR.

PART II.

OUR SAVIOUR.

CHRIST THE IMAGE OF GOD.

It is a distinguishing beauty of the Christian religion, that, while it teaches the purely spiritual character of our Creator, it presents to us, in Jesus, a copy of his moral perfections, suited to our comprehension, and worthy of our highest love and reverence. But for this, the Divine Being, in all the majesty of his infinite attributes, might have appeared too exalted even for our worship. Our thoughts, accustomed to the visible, corporeal objects around us, cannot long endure the contemplation of the invisible, incorporeal, infinite Mind. Hence, many nations have fallen into idolatry; either representing their Maker by some visible image, or worshipping instead some natural object, as the sun, the moon, or the stars. In the

Hebrew nation, how constantly were prophecies, miracles, chastisements, necessary to counteract a similar tendency! Yet they were provided with outward objects of reverence, in their temple and their ceremonial law. At length their tendency to idolatry was subdued; and in the heathen world, also, intellectual refinement had prepared the way for a spiritual religion. That religion was bestowed upon the world. But, spiritual as it is, it was beneficently adapted to human infirmity. While the Almighty remains, and ever must remain, exalted above our highest comprehension, he has graciously furnished us with an image of himself, in the character of Jesus; so that when our attention is overpowered in the contemplation of the Eternal Father, we may yet gaze, unwearied, on the "brightness of his glory," as it beams in milder lustre in the person of his holy messenger.

With this thought is to be connected another. Though the character of the Eternal be, in its fulness, far too high for our conceptions, yet the resemblance of that character exists, to some degree, in ourselves. We are made in the image of God; and, debased as our natures have been by our own sins, that image still exists in us. We could never understand any thing of the justice or the benevolence of God, did not justice and benevolence exist in ourselves. We conceive of every Divine attribute only by the possession of its likeness. The peculiarity, then, in the character of Jesus, which makes him to us a representative of the Father, is, that he was a perfect man, — that in him, this image, which to some degree exists in each of us, was found in perfection. In contemplating him, then, we are led to a fuller knowledge of the Divine character, while at the same time we view our own nature in that perfection which may be to ourselves the crown of eternal happiness in another world. He stood on earth, in human nature, indeed, but in human nature pure from sin, — in that human nature which reflects the glories of the Divine.

In confirmation of this view, let us contemplate his character more nearly, as delineated by the four Evangelists.

But to what point shall we turn? Even those who have denied his claim to a supernatural commission, acknowledge the loveliness, the glory, of that heavenly character; yet when we approach it, we stand surprised as well as awed. Its harmony prevents us, for a time, from understanding it. The man Christ Jesus is not like other men. The moment we think of others, with whose history we are familiar, their leading traits recur to our remembrance. With the name of Peter is connected inseparably the idea of impetuous zeal; the character of Paul is ever that of one formed to command; that of John exhibits one formed to love. But when we look to Jesus, what trait in him shall we select as shining above all the rest?

None! and this constitutes one of those moral miracles which so strongly assist the evidence to the truth of Christianity. The character of Jesus is not one which any person would have invented. It would have borne the impress of its fabricator. As it is, it bears the impress of heaven, and of heaven alone. Never man spake like that man; never man lived like him; never man died like him. Look at his character; — consider it well; then point out its peculiar grace. Is it the love of God and submission to him, revealed in the agony of the garden, and in his daily converse with the Supreme? But is his love to those around him less beautiful, manifested as it is in his long parting conversation, — manifested throughout his life, and at his death? And will you select these traits of character as bearing peculiarly the impress of superiority? Look yet again. The eye that wept over the tomb of Lazarus could awe, with a look that struck them backward to the earth, the soldiers who came to take him. The tongue that spoke such words of boundless love to his followers, struck terror to the consciences of the guilty Pharisees. He who humbled himself to wash the feet of his disciples, appeared equally in the majesty of heavenly perfection, whether he rode into Jerusalem amid the hosannas of the people, or stood a prisoner in the hall of the chief priest or of Pilate. The same being who prayed that the cup of sorrow might be taken from him, yet in submission to the will of Him who gave it, the same being it was who made those replies of patient dignity, — "If I have spoken evil, bear witness of the evil; but if well, why smitest thou me?" "Thou couldst have no power at all against me, except it were given thee from above." "Daughters of Jerusalem, weep not for me, but weep for yourselves and for your children." His character is a union of qualities seldom found together, never but in him found together in perfection. From this we may derive a most important lesson, that, in aiming at the purification and exaltation of our own characters, we should not make it our object to excel in one point or in a few points merely, but in all; and that we should never rest till the victory be gained, till we come to the stature of perfect men in Christ

Jesus, deficient in no part, but formed in beautiful proportion to the resemblance of our glorious model.

We thus contemplate in Jesus the image of Divine excellence, united, identified, with the perfection of human virtue. What a field for meditation is open before us here! In Jesus the Divine and human characters meet; through Jesus we learn that we are truly created in the image of God, for we see that image in him while we recognize him as one of our brethren. How important is the truth thus impressed! We are sharers in the Divine character; we are like God; — we may become more like him. Already are we like him in all that is worthiest, most elevated, in our principles and conduct; and that the resemblance may be increased, he has stamped this more perfect image of himself on a human being, and presents that being to us as the object of our love, and reverence, and imitation.

At length, we trust, a time will come when we shall be like our Saviour, " for we shall see him as he is." Then, in the nearer contemplation of Divine perfections, shall we attain that freedom from sin, that high degree of holiness, which constituted Jesus, and will constitute us, " the image of the Invisible God." Glorious, transcendent destiny! If men could but realize it, — if they had faith in what the Gospel teaches, — if they but believed and felt the sacred truth, that they are children of God, and are to become like their Father, and to live for ever with him, — how eagerly would they turn from the prizes of ambition, however bright, — from the pursuit of riches, however engrossing, — from sensual pleasure, however fascinating, — and think no labor, no privation, no endurance, too severe, so that their immortal hopes might be secured!

CHRIST OUR BROTHER.

WHATEVER views may be entertained by any with respect to the exalted character and office of our holy Master, all admit him to have been, in the most obvious sense, a brother of the great family of man. Like us he lay, a feeble infant, in his mother's arms; like us, he acquired, gradually, as month succeeded month, and year followed year, a knowledge of the objects around him; like ours, his young thoughts were strengthened by degrees, till able to take in the great idea of God. Like ours, too, his moral strength grew with his bodily and intellectual. As he "increased in wisdom and stature," so also "in favor with God and man." It was gradually that the innocence of childhood ripened into the virtue of perfected humanity. So, too, in after life, like us he became acquainted with the various forms of suffering by actual experience. He shared the pleasures and the pains of human nature. He was "found in fashion as a man," and was "made perfect through sufferings." "In all things it behooved him to be made like unto his brethren."

And as we regard his character as the standard of perfect humanity, we are not surprised to find that the feelings, which are often rudely checked and kept from their full development, were in him more strongly exhibited than they are in the majority of mankind. The susceptibility to pain, which made the anticipations in Gethsemane so agonizing to him, has been eagerly noticed by those who would rejoice to find something to censure in his holy character; — not perceiving that, the more agonizing was his idea of the tortures he was to undergo, the greater was the triumph of courage, love, and holiness in enduring them. The keenness with which every gentler emotion was felt by him has been often commented on, exhibited, as it was, in his last affectionate meeting with his disciples before his death, his friendship for the Apostle John, for Lazarus and his sisters, and his care, even in death, for the comfort and future home of his bereaved mother.

Nor is his participation in human nature and human feelings alone the ground on which we speak of the brotherhood of Christ with man. He exhibited to mankind a brother's love. Ever before his mind, probably from the earliest thoughtful hours of youth, was the great object of benefiting the human race, as that object has been before the minds of the wise and the holy, who have left names honored on the records of philanthropic exertion. Thus does the great English poet describe him, as communing with himself in meditation.

"When I was yet a child, no childish play
To me was pleasing; all my mind was set
Serious to learn and know, and thence to do
What might be public good: myself I thought
Born to that end, born to promote all truth."

"Victorious deeds
Flamed in my heart, heroic acts; one while
To rescue Israel from the Roman yoke,
Then to subdue and quell, o'er all the earth,
Brute violence and proud tyrannic power,
Till truth were freed and equity restored;
Yet held it more humane, more heavenly, first
By winning words to conquer willing hearts,
And make persuasion do the work of fear."
Paradise Regained, Book I.

We can well believe that the genius of Milton, itself so conversant with all that is high and noble, depicted rightly, in this passage, the early meditations of the Son of God, the Brother, the Friend, the Saviour of mankind. And conformable to such high anticipations, only more elevated still, as the maturity of a holy life exceeds the loftiest conception of it that youth can form, was the course which he actually pursued. Well is it said of him, that he "went about doing good." His supernatural powers were constantly exerted to relieve pain, and increase happiness; and not these alone. He was, wherever he went, the consoler of the afflicted, the rescuer of the fallen, the rebuker, and thus in truth the friend, of those who sinned through hypocrisy and pride. Yes, to the Pharisee, as to the publican, Jesus came as a friend; — if his language was stern, it was a salutary sternness, and the difference of his reception by the two classes was not from partiality in him, but from unworthiness on the part of those who rejected him. But his immediate intercourse with those around him, whether in healing their outward infirmities, or ministering to their spiritual wants, constituted but a small part of the benefits he conferred upon mankind. Only by a portion of the inhabitants of the small country of Judea was his voice directly heard; only to a smaller number among them were his blessings of outward healing wrought; but to the millions of the civilized world, for age after age, has he administered comfort in sorrow, strength for duty, salvation from sin and from its consequent misery. Christ came with a brother's love, not to those around him only, not to Israel alone, but to the human race.

This reflection may enable us to enter in some degree into the grandeur of our Saviour's thoughts. He is standing by the couch of one whom he has raised from death, the daughter of the ruler, Jairus. The Apostles look on in awe at the display of Divine power and benignity; the parents of the child are prostrate at his feet in thankfulness, then turn to clasp their recovered treasure to their breasts. Gratitude, love, and reverence fill the hearts of all, and for what blessing? That he has rescued one child from the early grave to which she was to be consigned in her innocence, that he has recalled her to life, with its many trials, its certain temptations, its uncertain results to human happiness and virtue. Amid the group of the thankful ones stands the Saviour, receiving benignantly their words of gratitude; but are his thoughts alone with them? No; his mental sight surveys the thousands upon thousands then unborn, who should, through that and other signs of his Divine mission, be brought to faith in him, and through faith to blessedness here and hereafter. As he hath raised this child, so, he feels, shall his followers — a company whom no man can number — be raised at the last day. As he looks on the mother, weeping with joy at the restoration of the child for whom she had been weeping more bitter tears, does there not come to him the thought, how many a mother, through ages yet to come, should find consolation in similar distress, by the knowledge which he had brought of the character of God and of the truth of a resurrection?

There is something peculiarly beautiful in the guidance which a virtuous elder brother exercises for the younger members of the family; and it deserves to be compared with the relation of our Saviour to his disciples. There is in such a one a blending of authority and gentleness; a power, whose origin is in love and wisdom; a feeling of sympathy, as well as of superiority. How truly is this displayed in the intercourse between our Lord and his disciples! He was their companion; the journey which proved too wearisome for his bodily powers had tasked theirs also; at the meal of which they partook, he broke the bread and gave thanks; some of them were with him in his hour of glory on the Mount of Transfiguration, and in his hour of sorrow in Gethsemane. But with this near companionship there was a reverence deep in proportion. More than once it withheld them from asking him the meaning of words which had seemed mysterious. They called him Master and Lord, and he could say to them, with the calm dignity of conscious worth, "Ye say well, for so I am." Thus were the two constituents of the relation we have spoken of, as existing between an older brother and the younger members of the family, of whom he is the guide, united in the intercourse of the disciples with Christ, — intimate companionship and affection, with respectful deference. And thus, too, we, as we meditate on Christ, draw near to him in spirit, and perceive those qualities in his sacred character that win an affection, a tender regard, resembling that which binds us to our best-beloved earthly brethren, while, at the same time, deep, heartfelt reverence leads us to look up to him, as the holiest of the sons of God, — that God who is the Father of us all.

Probably there is no scene in which Jesus showed himself the brother of mankind more truly, or in a more beautiful manner, than when he returned to Judea, to the midst of his enemies, and sought out the place where the body of Lazarus had been laid. His personal affection to the friend whom he had lost, and to the sisters, brought out in a clear light the tenderness of his nature. He showed himself there truly and in the highest sense a man, sympathizing with human griefs, comforting human sorrows; while even in his tears there is nothing extravagant, nothing inconsistent with the dignity of his sublime office. The consummation of that scene, the raising of Lazarus from the dead, filled with awe and gratitude the minds of the spectators; but to us, who see that great transaction through the mists of time, the exhibition of true human feeling, blended with heavenly faith, in his preceding language and deportment, is more impressive than when we are told that he who was dead came forth from the tomb.

Christ, then, is our brother. "He that sanctifieth and they who are sanctified are all of one" Father; "for which cause he is not ashamed to call them brethren." This name, too, he gave to those who should obey his word, on that occasion when his relatives sought to hold converse with him, in order, probably, to withdraw him from what they thought his too great engrossment with the duties of his office. "Who," said he, "is my mother, and who are my brethren? And he looked round about upon his disciples and said, Behold my mother and my brethren; for whosoever shall do the will of God and keep it, the same is my brother, and sister, and mother."

Where there is brotherhood, there is similarity of nature and of powers; the difference is in degree, not in kind. Where, then, our brother hath been, there we may follow. Temptations which he met and vanquished, we may aspire to vanquish also, in the strength imparted by that God who is his Father, and ours. The glorious crown which he won, transcendent in radiance as it is, is not all unlike the celestial diadems which are to wreathe the brows of those who follow in the path he first trod. We are encouraged to contemplate his character more nearly, when we know that its perfections are such as our minds are adequate to contemplate, — such as we ourselves may more or less nearly at length resemble.

The thought carries us into the future world. If even here below, we are, if we strive to do God's will, recognized by Christ as his brethren, how much more truly may that exalted relationship be the object of our anticipations, in connection with the happiness of heaven! There, — we are told by one of our elder brethren, his Apostles, — there we shall be like him, for we shall see him as he is. Well may the result follow from the nearer communion, the enlarged power of vision and of understanding, with which we shall then be favored. Then shall our present doubts and differences, respecting his station in the universe of his Father, be removed; the knowledge with regard to his character, which we can here derive only from meditation on the accounts of the Evangelists and Apostles, may there be increased by more full revelations. Then, too, the fascinating enjoyments of earth, the temptations of sin, will be removed; and, these withdrawn, we shall be more able to contemplate and admire the most glorious of all objects, moral loveliness. Then, to our purified and quickened sight shall be displayed, far more than here on earth, the great designs which Jesus had in view in what he did, and taught, and suffered; and we shall see the depth and fulness of that love which gave itself for us. As we behold, can we but strive for resemblance? Ours then shall be, if here we patiently and humbly strive to do God's will, through ages without end on high, the rapture of ever-increasing resemblance in character to our glorious model, while, with each approach, still closer and closer will be drawn the band of that affection which unites our spirits to their glorified Brother, the Son of God, the Saviour of the world.

CHRIST OUR EXAMPLE.

THERE is one peculiarity in our Saviour's moral excellence, which, in the view of many, prevents the full application of his example to our use. It is this. The stainless virtue of the Saviour, we are told, is accounted for by his peculiar connection with the Father. Setting aside the question which has been so much discussed, of his possessing a share in the Divine nature, — setting aside, also, the doctrine of his preëxistence, as an archangelic being, — he was, as man alone, privileged with an intercourse with the Most High, such as has been granted to no other among the children of men. The intimacy of that intercourse is expressed in his own words, that "no man knoweth the Son but the Father, and no man knoweth the Father save the Son, and he to whom the Son will reveal him"; — in the repeated assertions that he came from God and went to God, and the strong expression that he and the Father are one. It is implied, too, in the miraculous power which he exercised, and in the knowledge he constantly evinced respecting the designs which the Almighty intended to accomplish by his instrumentality. How, it is asked, can a being thus exalted be an example to us? How can we, weak, ignorant creatures, to whom the Almighty has never directly revealed himself by vision or by miracle, whose rebellious passions have never been awed into silence by the manifest presence of the Holiest One, be called to follow the steps — say rather the heavenward flight — of this divinely privileged Son of God? Would it not be as reasonable to expect the savage to imitate the profound calculations of a Newton?

How shall we meet this difficulty? We cannot but admit its apparent importance, yet we perceive considerations of various kinds that may be urged to prove that still the example of Jesus, lofty and divine as it is, may rightly be held up before us as the mark of our aspirations, and of our reasonable hope, too, for resemblance.

In the first place, let it be remembered that there is a wide difference between the effort necessary to lead where the path is yet unknown, and that which is required in order to follow. We admire the genius of the great navigator who first crossed the ocean, and revealed to astonished Europe the existence of this New World. But that voyage once made, that knowledge once communicated, was any remarkable genius needed in each of the numerous adventurers who followed the track of the world-finder? The comparison has been made of the Christian following his Master's example to the savage vainly called on to imitate the scientific investigations of a Newton. But the sublimest discoveries of Newton are now familiar to thousands. So with the great subject we would illustrate. Before the time of Christ, revengeful feelings were indulged by those who were regarded as the holiest men. David, whose Psalms give proof of a heart full of the most glowing love and devotion toward God, yet spared not the bitterest imprecations against his own personal enemies, and probably never thought that any future age would see aught in such sentiments to condemn. But listen to the Saviour on the cross! For the first time the world hears, instead of a curse upon successful enemies, a prayer for them. "Father! forgive them, for they know not what they do." The glorious example is set, and set once for all. The words once heard, all perceive their sublimity, and many are capable of sufficient elevation to take them upon their lips and in their hearts. The very first follower of the Saviour who was put to death in his cause, the Martyr Stephen, could die with the same sentiment on his tongue, — "Lord, lay not this sin to their charge"; and hundreds, if not thousands, since his time, have probably done the same. So much easier is it to follow a glorious example than originally to exhibit it to the world.

This reflection, we may remark, in passing, while it encourages us to regard the imitation of our Saviour as attainable, gives us a more exalted idea of the perfections of our sacred model, and a cheering view of the influence which his life has already exerted on mankind. The example of Christ has elevated human kind in general. Some of the lessons he has taught us, we cannot unlearn if we would. Those who are careless about his religion, those who disbelieve it, are the better for its instructions. Every one now knows that the earth turns round on its axis; every one knows that it is noble to forgive injuries; and, as thousands who never heard of Galileo believe the scientific truth he taught, so thousands are profited by the teaching and example of Christ who acknowledge no allegiance to his religion.

Our second answer to the objection brought against the practicableness of our Lord's example is, that, sublime as was the intercourse with God that he enjoyed, we possess something corresponding. Of our Saviour's intercourse with God, some portion must apparently have related to the truths he was to teach, and the conduct he was to observe in connection with his high and peculiar office. This extraordinary and sublime communication of the Godhead may have been entirely different from any thing which we share or of which we have an idea. But not so was the communication between him and his Heavenly Father, which he enjoyed as an individual simply, apart from his official character. We read of his praying, and we, too, can pray. We read that the spirit was given to him, not by measure; we know that it is bestowed on us, if we seek it aright, though more sparingly. The difference, we have reason to believe, is not of kind, but of degree, except so far as related to our Lord's public duties. What was peculiar in his inspiration was for a peculiar purpose; but those Divine supports on which rested his holy human character may, to a great extent, be ours.

If, then, we are told that the example of Jesus is too lofty for us to imitate, we reply, in his own words, "With men it is impossible, but not with God." "Will not our Heavenly Father give his good spirit unto them that ask him?"

There is another consideration, which may be brought to illustrate the application of our Saviour's example to ourselves. Though his advantages for attaining high virtue were far greater than ours, his trials were also greater. This is in conformity to the general laws of moral discipline. The more we attain, the more we have still before us, as the traveller towards the heart of a mountainous region sees each successive ridge arise before him loftier than the one he has just surmounted. "To whom much is given, of him is much required." It is this truth that equalizes this world, as a state of probation for all, whether outwardly more or less favored. It is this, too, which makes it continue a state of probation to us, however highly we may have attained. Every new trust acquired has its corresponding responsibleness; every assurance that our conduct gives to those around us of our worth, leads them to look to us with firmer hope for the future; and, if at last we fail, renders our failure more melancholy. If, then, we must admit that the directness of our Saviour's intercourse with God, and the knowledge which he possessed of his own wonderful destiny, were safeguards to his virtue in which we cannot share, let us observe, also, the circumstances which exposed that virtue to trials never endured by us. The most obvious of these circumstances were the danger which threatened him from the steady opposition of his most influential countrymen, a danger which he well knew would finally become fatal; the remorseless and unprincipled nature, too, of that opposition, which might have tempted another to forget his own dignity and the claims of duty in the excitement of a personal contest; the allurements, too, of ambition, in the general wish of his hearers that he should become the champion, the deliverer, of his people. But these temptations, this last, especially, were immeasurably increased by the character of the powers he possessed. The authority over nature, which apparently was confided to others only in particular instances, was, if we rightly understand the language of Scripture, intrusted to him to an indefinite degree. The most striking assurance of this is where he told his followers, at the moment of his arrest, that he could even then pray to his Father and receive the aid of more than twelve legions of angels; adding, "But how then shall the Scriptures be fulfilled, that thus it must be?" His power, then, was discretionary. And, reasoning from analogy, we may conclude that his choice of means and plans of action was, to a great degree, discretionary also. Unless we believe this, we must regard him as less a free agent in his mighty work than any uninspired reformer in his humbler sphere. What a view of our Lord's power, and of his self-denial in the use thereof, do these considerations present! What a view, also, of the greatness of the temptations which he had to subdue! He was made king of the world, — animate and inanimate. The thrones of earth were at his command. Nay, more, it needed not, in order to attain any degree of earthly triumph, that he should renounce his high office as teacher of mankind, or prove distinctly unfaithful to his charge. Invested at discretion with these most lofty powers, the question was for him to decide how he was to use them for the best interest of mankind. He had it in his choice to bless the world as a conqueror, as a peaceful though prosperous king, or as a victim. He had the guidance, indeed, of those prophecies which intimated the suffering that marked his course, and of the spirit of God to illuminate and strengthen. But with his power, and with the choice left to himself how he should exert it, the temptation must have been strong indeed. He was so aware of its strength, that he appears to have felt, as with our less temptations we should feel, that safety lay in not for one moment listening to it. Hence the sternness of his rebuke to that disciple who ventured to remonstrate on his chosen course. "Get thee behind me, adversary, thou art a cause of sin to me; for thou savorest not the things that be of God, but the things that be of man." If, then, we feel that our Lord possessed spiritual aids that we cannot share, let us remember, also, that trials and temptations were his, far beyond any that we are called to encounter.

The same truth may be illustrated in a different manner. The higher man ascends in virtue, the more his delicacy of conscience increases. Things which at first appeared innocent to him, now, regarded by a purer sight, are classed among those which he must avoid. The aspiration of the mere novice in the Christian character may go no higher than to avoid dishonesty, profane language, and other of the grosser and more obvious faults. As he becomes more advanced, he learns to appreciate the duty of regulating his language by the rules of consideration and kindness, and exercising watchfulness over his thoughts. Thus we find the case to be in the imperfect degrees of virtue we are here privileged to attain; and we have reason to believe, that, in those higher acquisitions which our Saviour made, the law was still the same; — that the exquisite delicacy of his conscience recognized distinctions between right and wrong that are imperceptible to us, and that thus the spiritual aid he received was no more than proportioned to the occasion he found for its use.

If the views we have taken be correct, our Holy Redeemer, with all his supernatural powers, was yet a fitting model for tempted mortals; for he, too, was tempted. He, too, was called to wage a continual war against inducements that were presented to him to withdraw him in some degree from that sublime service which he undertook. But he resisted every temptation, chose and retained the path of the sufferer when he might have trod in that of universal empire, and set to mankind the example of sinlessness, — the most perfect in holiness of all God's children. We perceive, also, that, this example once set, to follow it is a far easier task, as the humblest student may now tread in the path of Newton, and the obscurest navigator can follow in the track of Columbus. The example of Jesus, then, is practical. It is not too high for man to aspire to be like him. Nor is it perfect resemblance which the justice of God, tempered by his mercy, demands of us. If the endeavour be sincere, the spirit humble, and the faith devout, deficiencies will be forgiven. With that high example, then, in view, with so much to aid our path and to show us the greater difficulties that beset our Saviour's, shall we fail to strive for the prize of holiness which he has shown us how to win? Let us resolve, like him, to serve our God and our race; like him, to suffer no earthly hope or fear to stand between us and duty; like him, to love and aid even those by whom we have been unjustly treated; like him, even in the hour of life's parting anguish, to bow meekly to the will of God, to comfort the distress of friends, to relieve and support the spirit of the trembling penitent, and pray for our Father's blessing, even on our enemies.

CHRIST'S ANTICIPATIONS.

As our Redeemer drew near to the closing scenes of his ministry, the thought of all that was to come appears to have been constantly present to his mind. Did the grateful Mary pour ointment on his head? He referred the act, though occurring in the hour of festivity, to his approaching burial. Did Gentile strangers seek an interview with him? He replied to the disciple who brought their request, "The hour is come that the Son of man should be glorified," and then turned from the thought of glory to that of death.* We may enter more fully into the Saviour's feelings, by taking a brief view of those objects which presented themselves to his prophetic anticipation.

The event most distinctly before his mind was death, from which, under nearly all circumstances,

* John xii. 3–7; 20–27.

human nature shrinks with loathing and dread. It was death, too, in a form at once the most detested, from the infamy it usually implied, and abhorred, from the complication of bodily pain which attended it. Of all the torments which bloody man has invented for his fellow-man, none, probably, has implied more of suffering than crucifixion. It was a lingering death; though, in the case of our Redeemer, its pangs were far shorter than in most instances, yet with him the agony of the constrained position, the lacerated flesh, the burning limbs, the scorching thirst, endured about three hours. Nor was this all; previous to these tortures, which drove out life, the sufferer bore the infliction of the scourge, with the accompanying insults of a brutal soldiery, and then was obliged to carry the cross to the spot where the execution was to take place. This burden was so heavy, that the strength of our Saviour sank under it, and his guards obliged a traveller whom they met to aid in sustaining it. With all this immediate bodily suffering was united the peculiarly disgraceful nature of the punishment. The cross is to us a hallowed emblem; but when our Saviour endured its weight and its tortures, the cross was known but as the most disgraceful and most painful means of inflicting the punishment of death. It was reserved for the vilest of malefactors, and for slaves. Such was the death to which the holy Son of God submitted. Such was the fate he had in view, when, steadfastly banishing every weaker thought, he exclaimed, "Father, glorify thy name!"

His was no sudden act of self-devotion, made in a moment of excitement, when there was not time to appreciate the full greatness of the sufferings to be endured. No. From the first, the dark future was placed before his mind. But his choice was deliberately and unchangeably made. He did not relax the sternness of his denunciations against the hypocrite, though, while denouncing him, he well knew the implacable and fatal enmity he was exciting against himself. But his reliance was on stronger principles, — the sense of duty, the love of mankind, the love of God.

And to the pains of death, to the tortures of anticipation, another sting was added, by the thought to whose enmity his death was owing. The feeling of patriotism had its place, with every other worthy and exalted emotion, in our Saviour's breast. He loved his country, — Israel, the chosen land and the chosen people of God. He loved Jerusalem, the city of the Great King, the place where only, throughout the world, a temple rose and an altar flamed to the worship of the One True God. He loved his fellow-countrymen; he would willingly have gathered them beneath his protection, and beneath the forgiving mercy and love of his Father. He wept at the thought of their approaching calamities. He was their brother according to the flesh. He was the lineal descendant of their ancient kings, — of David and Solomon, whose reigns had been the period of their highest political and spiritual glory. He was the Messiah whom they had so long expected, and in whom they looked to see that ancient glory restored. And he had come to accomplish the prophecies, to fulfil the hopes of his people, to shed on Israel and on the world the blessings of a true and pure religion. Now he was to die; and who were to be the authors of his death? Those very men whom he had come to bless and to save. It was Israel that had rejected her Saviour. It was Jerusalem that clamored for the crucifixion of her king. It was they for whose good he had labored and prayed, over whose obduracy he had wept, — they whom he loved as fellow-countrymen, as brethren, as the subjects of that earthly sceptre which he might have claimed, and of that higher authority which belonged to him as the Anointed Messenger of God, — it was these to whom he owed his death. The feeling of this added acuteness to his suffering. He saw their ingratitude, their obstinacy. He felt deeply the pang inflicted by this return of evil for the good he had bestowed. But even this conquered not his love of country. On the cross itself he prayed for the forgiveness of his countrymen, on the ground of ignorance. "Father, forgive them, for they know not what they do." The very knowledge how fearfully Providence would avenge his death, added another pang to his sufferings. It was with no exultation in his tone, that he exclaimed, "Daughters of Jerusalem, weep not for me, but weep for yourselves and for your children." He saw, in prophetic anticipation, the scenes which were shortly to take place. He saw the vine-covered hills and smiling plains of his beloved Galilee desolated with fire, and the march of invading armies. He beheld her flourishing and populous cities levelled with the ground, and the placid and beautiful lake which had been honored by his miracles and his instructions dyed with the blood of thousands massacred on its banks. He saw the royal and holy city, Jerusalem, compassed with armies, and its own inhabitants, more fierce than their invaders, turning their hands against each other; without, instead of the three crosses on Calvary, thousands, on which the exasperated Roman executed his prisoners; within, the combined ravages of discord, plague, and famine, — the mother herself, as we are told, in some instances sustaining life upon the flesh of her own offspring. He saw the Temple, the sacred spot where God's honor dwelt, wrapped in flames, while, amid bursting arches and falling porticos, the battle still raged on between the conquering Roman and the perishing remnant of Judah. Thirty-eight years after the death of Jesus these things took place. They were the consequences of a war, in which the nation never would and never could have engaged, had they adopted the peaceful religion of Jesus for their guide. These were, then, in God's providence, the awful consequences attendant on their rejection of him. To these he looked forward; the anticipation of these miseries of his country added bitterness to the cup of suffering he was compelled to taste. Even for the guilty he could pray; and he knew how, in a season of such universal calamity, the innocent would be involved with the guilty in a common doom.

And how must his heart have sunk within him as he thought of what his disciples, his friends, were to endure! He left them, — those who had been the companions of his labors, those who had loved and honored him, and over whom he had watched with answering love; the enthusiastic Peter, the mild and affectionate John, and every other member of that small but endeared company,— he left them, and to what? To a course of usefulness, indeed, and of glory, but a course of suffering; to the enmity alike of their own countrymen and of the Gentiles; to temptations by which their strength would be painfully tried, and beneath which he knew that sometimes and for a season it would fail. We can imagine the mournfulness in his tone, as he said to Peter, "Verily I say unto thee, thou shalt deny me thrice"; as he said to the disciples, "All ye shall be offended because of me this night." But he foresaw that these temptations, these failures of strength, would be but transitory. He trusted, he knew by the intercourse of his spirit with that of God, that from every failure his Apostles would rise with renewed vigor. Still more sad, then, may have been his anticipation of the external calamities they would be called to experience. He foresaw the painful journeys they must undertake, the contumely, the oppression, the tumultuous assaults, to which they must be subjected. He saw the hand of Herod stretched out to vex the Church, and James, the brother of John, falling a victim to his fury. He looked farther along the stream of time, and saw the death of one glorious martyr after another; the crucifixion of Peter, the beheading of Paul; the still fiercer rage which was kindled in the breasts of heathen rulers, as they saw their altars gradually deserted, and their subjects embracing the cause of the Redeemer. Persecution after persecution he foresaw; he declared that it would be so, when he said, "I came not to send peace on earth, but a sword." And darker still than the prospect of the sufferings his disciples would endure must have been that of the crimes they would commit. How much more keenly must the iron have entered into his soul, as he saw his own Church rent in sunder, and its respective parties persecuting one another even to the death! Such were the alternating causes of joy and sorrow, which crowded into our Saviour's breast as he contemplated the effects of his death, in the progress of his religion in the world.

He had felt as a friend, he was called to feel also as a son. That earliest friend, his mother, whose parental care his blameless infancy and his holy youth had repaid with a fulness of love and happiness such as never fell to the lot of any parent but her,—that mother, worthy of the high honor of giving birth to the Redeemer, he was to leave, mourning and desolate. The thought of her found attention amidst his dying agonies on the cross ; he commended her, in almost his latest breath, to the care of the disciple whom he loved, and received comfort in the knowledge that his request would be well complied with. "From that hour that disciple took her unto his own home."

But the prospect before the mind of our Saviour was not altogether gloomy. Above the dark picture of the ruin of his country, and the sufferings of his friends, appeared the radiant dawn of pure religion upon the world. Our Lord knew the greatness of the cause in which he was to die. He knew that through his death that cause would triumph. His prophetic eye glanced over the course of his Apostles, their trials, their exertions, their success. He surveyed in spirit the extension of his religion from city to city, from land to land, its triumph over heathenism, its establishment through the world. We may believe, too, that his spirit was cheered by the assurance of that high intercourse which he afterwards maintained with his Apostles. He foresaw, it may be, that, though removed from them in bodily presence, it would still be granted him to influence them by an agency exerted upon their minds, and at times to reveal himself, as he did to Stephen and to Paul, by miraculous visions. High and rapturous must have been the contemplation of his approaching glory; higher and more rapturous to his holy mind, because with his own was united the glory of his Father. Wherever his doctrine should prevail, there he knew that the God from whom he came would be worshipped in spirit and in truth. With what emotions, then, of filial joy in the advancement of his Father's honor, with what benevolent exultation in the good of mankind, must he have looked forward to the time when the pure and blessed religion introduced by him should be extended through the earth, — when the throne of the All-Holy should be established in every heart!

For whom did Jesus die? For mankind. For those whom he had not seen. For the unworthy, as well as for the virtuous. For us. Yes; we are of the number of those for whom that precious blood was shed. We are among those over whom his prophetic vision passed, as among the thousands of millions who should receive through him the glad tidings of salvation. To us, then, comes the call of gratitude for what he suffered. "Greater love hath no man than this, that a man lay down his life for his friends."

CHRIST IN GETHSEMANE.

Our Saviour possessed human nature in its perfection. Every faculty, every perception, was perfect; and, not less than others, those perceptions which recognize the presence of painful and terrifying objects. It was in the garden of Gethsemane that this portion of his mental constitution was called to its most agonizing trial. He felt there as man must ever feel when, in the stillness of midnight and solitude, in communion only with God and his own heart, he meditates on the approach of a painful and seemingly disgraceful death. Many have thought the emotion which the Saviour now exhibited too great to be accounted for from this cause alone. They have supposed that, at this awful hour, he endured some terrors connected more mysteriously with the high objects of his mission; — that it was now that he felt the burden of that vast sum of human transgression, for which his death was to make atonement before God; — that the terrors of the powers of hell were around him, and awful suggestions harassing his soul, while the favoring countenance of God no longer beamed upon him, but instead thereof he saw himself the object, for a season, of the Divine displeasure, which was transferred to him from the human race. We cannot admit the correctness of these views in their full latitude, while, instead of fiends tormenting him, we read that there appeared unto him an angel strengthening him, and while we feel that, instead of then experiencing the Divine displeasure, the holy Jesus can at no period of his course have received more fully the approbation of the Most High than he did amid the agony, the humiliation, the self-sacrifice, of that moment. And yet it may well be believed that the thought which came upon him, of the immense importance of that self-offering which he was then presenting, had something in it calculated to overwhelm the soul. He felt that on his endurance depended consequences not to be limited by the lapse of ages. The human race, for countless unborn generations, were to be sharers in the joy that he should communicate; — and what if, in the last awful hour, his strength were to fail, and the perfect example of patient suffering were to be sullied by a single blot? Is it too much to imagine that he, who all admit was perfect man,—he who "was tempted in all points as we are,"—felt this supposition pass through his mind, and shrunk and trembled under his great responsibleness, as he thought of the possibility that he might not sustain it? Does it not seem as if some mental struggle of this kind was indicated in the words he used to his disciples?—"Pray that ye enter not into temptation; the spirit truly is willing, but the flesh is weak." Did he mean to suggest to them a warning, from the fearful nature of that trial, which even he had scarcely been able to bear?

But whatever we may fancy, who shall pretend to fathom thoroughly the feelings which passed through that pure and glorious soul in its hour of deepest affliction? Their result was expressed in the prayer, "Father, if thou be willing, let this cup pass from me; nevertheless, not my will, but thine, be done." The first sentence of that prayer was the expression of those natural feelings which have been commented on. We may view it as something more; as a last solemn act of humility, in laying down before the throne of his Father his mediatorial crown, divesting himself of the high office of Redeemer of the world, so far as he might consistently with duty, that he might assume it again, not of his own will, but of the will of his Father, — not depending on his own strength, but on the strength of his Father. If we may venture to express the sentiments of that prayer more at large, thus might we interpret it. "Father, thou hast committed to me a task of fearful magnitude; I have assumed it in obedience to thy will; and now I stand about to enter on that scene of insult and suffering, before which my soul sinks in utter dismay. How shall I endure that which is before me? How shall I pass through this more than fiery trial, without obscuring, by any deficiency, the brightness of that example which thy chosen one must leave to his disciples through all ages to come? O Father, the spirit is willing to obey thee, but the flesh, the love of life, and every feeling which thou hast impressed on this human nature, — these shrink from that awful duty; and I shrink, too, from that worse fear, that I may possibly fail in its full discharge. Father! if it be thy will, I would lay down before thee the office thou hast given. But thy will, not mine, be done."

"Nevertheless, not as I will, but as thou wilt." Here was at length the triumph of faith, and love to God and man, and glorious self-devotion, over every doubt and every fear. This language was not a mere profession, without corresponding meaning. It was not a form of words, adopted from distant antiquity, or even from any single previous example, to express a resignation which was not felt. It conveyed the sincere and entire submission of his own will to the will of God. And in that submission the Saviour found a renewal of strength and peace. The worst struggle was now over, — the bitterness of death was in a great measure past; the patient Son of God was prepared to endure, in the strength of his Father, what was yet to be laid upon him of suffering, abuse, and death.

THE ARREST, TRIAL, AND CRUCIFIXION.

THE narrative of the sufferings of Jesus has been a thousand times repeated, but it has not lost, and can never lose, its interest to his followers. Let us trace, step by step, the successive incidents of those affecting scenes.

From the agonizing struggle, and the prayer of self-renunciation, our Lord returned to his disciples, whom he had left to await him at a short distance. He found them, we are told, "sleeping for sorrow." Had they been aware, like him, of the immediate approach of danger, excitement would have banished sleep; but theirs was only the saddened feeling produced by witnessing in him a grief, the cause of which they could but imperfectly understand, and this feeling rather aided than resisted the influence of fatigue and darkness. He aroused them, saying that the hour of his betrayal had come. His words were fulfilled while yet upon his lips. A multitude approached, led by Judas, who knew the place to which his Master was accustomed to resort. The traitor designates his Lord by a kiss, the abused mark of love and confidence; and the Saviour himself comes forward and declares that he is the man they seek. The soldiers, though awed at first by the calm majesty of his demeanour, make him their prisoner. Peter attempts a vain resistance, but the Saviour forbids it, and performs, even in that moment, a miracle of mercy, healing the wound which his ardent disciple had made. He desires of his captors, in surrendering himself, that those with him should not be detained. Self-collected at that trying moment, he remembers and fulfils every duty. He notices, too, with deep feeling, those circumstances of his capture which were most revolting, — the treacherous kiss, and the arrest by an armed multitude at night, when ample opportunity had been given for the summons of a legal officer. "Judas, betrayest thou the Son of Man with a kiss?" "Be ye come out against a thief, with swords and staves? When I was daily with you in the temple, ye stretched forth no hands against me; but this is your hour, and the power of darkness."

He was taken first, probably by previous orders

from Caiaphas, to the house of Annas, the father-in-law and predecessor of the high-priest. Annas, it is conjectured, could not, on account of age, be present with those assembled in the house of Caiaphas; and the sanction of his authority was desired for the course which they intended to pursue. However this may have been, the aged magistrate appears to have at once referred the case to his son-in-law, Caiaphas, the actual possessor of the high priesthood; and to his house Jesus was next conducted.

Here he was examined, though apparently in an irregular manner, the formal meeting of the Sanhedrim not taking place till the morning. In the mean time, however, witnesses were sought and heard against him, and he was subjected to insult and abuse. It was during this interval, too, that his ear caught, from the outer room, the excited tones of a well-known voice, the voice of the most ardent of his friends, denying with oaths that he knew him. This he had himself foretold, yet the fulfilment added bitterness to the cup of misery.

In the morning the council assembled and passed their sentence; but the power was not theirs to carry it into effect. That power resided with the Roman governor, and to him the prisoner was now led.

Brought before Pilate, the Saviour is questioned upon the charge made against him, of aspiring to the name and authority of a king. He asserts, in reply, his claim to that title, but qualifies the declaration with the words, "My kingdom is not of this world." "To this end was I born, and for this cause came I into the world, that I should bear witness unto the truth." "What is truth?" exclaims the governor, apparently with contemptuous indifference. But he appears to have been satisfied, by the answers of Jesus, that he was neither a guilty nor a dangerous person. The Jews, however, are clamorous for his death, and Pilate avails himself of the suggestion that the prisoner belonged to Galilee, to refer the case to Herod, prince of that province, then on a visit to Jerusalem. By Herod he is sent back to Pilate, arrayed in a purple robe, in mockery of his supposed pretensions to royalty. The better feelings of the governor struggle long against his timid and unprincipled policy, and that very struggle does but increase the torture of the Divine sufferer, who is scourged and crowned with thorns, that the compassion of the people may be excited in his favor. At length Pilate yields, and the Saviour is led forth, bearing his cross. As he passes along, nearly fainting under his dreadful burden, a traveller (we may imagine) stops and regards the victim with an eye of pity, or utters some exclamation that betrays his feelings. He is seized by the soldiers, and compelled to aid in bearing the cross.

They move on. But now the company who trod that which should for ever after be called the Dolorous Way, was swelled by the accession of the friends of Jesus, and the women who, to the lasting glory of their sex, had thus far honored and now bewailed him. To these he addresses a few words, of awfully prophetic import, referring, but not vindictively, to the miseries that were to come upon his country from those Romans by whose hands he was now to die. On reaching Calvary, "they gave him vinegar to drink, mingled with gall." This was a stupefying draught, provided by the rude mercy of the age, to diminish the pangs of that fearful mode of execution. But "when he had tasted thereof, he would not drink." No cloud must be upon his faculties, to obscure the vision of the opening heaven, and dim the brightness of his dying example.

His first words when on the cross, and in the recent agony of his wounds, were, "Father! forgive them; for they know not what they do." Is it too much to say that these are the most sublime words ever uttered by man? Jesus had taught the lesson, "Love your enemies," and men had marvelled, as they marvel now, that he should deliver a precept so impossible to observe. He now showed that the glorious soul that could conceive the law was capable also of its fulfilment.

Again he speaks; and they are words of comfort to the penitent offender at his side.

Again; and it is with the care of a son for the mother who never till now had known the meaning of those words, "Yea, a sword shall pierce through thine own soul also." Mary! "highly favored among women!"—were the angelic announcement, the early signs and wonders, the sinless childhold, the holy youth, the divine maturity, all to end in this? Retain thy faith, mother of the Saviour! He remembers thee in this hour of his own agony and thine; think not, then, that he can be abandoned by his God and Father!

And yet what means that startling cry? "My God, my God, why hast thou forsaken me?" Fear not; those words from his lips no more imply distrust, than they did in the earnest pleading of that psalm which the sufferer now applies to his own condition.

The agony of the cross produces its usual effect, excessive thirst; and Jesus, who had never taught, like the Stoics, that there was virtue in an affected insensibility to pain, expresses that feeling. It is relieved by tasting, not of the drugged beverage offered him before, but of vinegar alone.

"When Jesus therefore had received the vinegar, he said, It is finished; and he bowed his head, and gave up the ghost."

PART III.

THE COMMUNICANT.

PART III.

THE COMMUNICANT.

SELF-EXAMINATION.

I AM now about to unite with my fellow-disciples in the act of commemorating our Redeemer. Let me consider the meaning of what I do, and, as the Apostle has directed, "examine myself," before I "eat of that bread and drink of that cup."

It is an ordinance of profession. Has my conduct been worthy of the religion I profess? Father, who knowest my sins, grant that I may see them in their true light, may turn from them, and hereafter walk more worthily before thee!

It is an ordinance of commemoration. Have I kept in memory my Saviour's law, and the example by which it was illustrated? Has the light of his character been reflected from mine?

It is an ordinance of love to him. It reminds me of his love to mankind, displayed in his death. How shall I best manifest my own in return? He hath said, "If ye love me, keep my commandments."

It is a communion, a feast of brotherly love. "By this shall all men know that ye are my disciples, if ye have love one to another." Have I exhibited, not to man alone, but to God, this mark of a true discipleship?

It is an occasion for grateful feeling to that God who sent Jesus on earth. Is my gratitude manifested by my life? Have I "ceased to do evil"? Do I "learn to do well"?

Let me take for my guidance, in self-examination, the Ten Commandments of God's ancient law, applying them, as extended and illustrated by the Gospel, to my own conduct and spiritual condition.

I. Have I any "other gods" before Jehovah? Is there any object to whose service I have bound myself more than to his? Is eagerness for wealth or distinction leading me away from duty? Have I been led into idolatry by the warmth of my affections, or do I hold even my dearest treasures in humility, as subject to His will who gave them, and can resume?

II. Do I serve God after the right manner, or as they of old time worshipped him by unworthy emblems, do I render to him such tribute as cannot be pleasing in his sight? Does the feeling of sectarian bitterness mingle with my zeal for truth, or is my worship tainted with formalism, hypocrisy, or superstition?

III. Have I guarded my lips against irreverence of expression? Do I suppress, as it rises in my thoughts, the misapplication of Scripture, and every word that may diminish the regard of others, or my own, for sacred things? Am I faithful, in letter and in spirit, to every vow that I have taken, every obligation that I have assumed in the sight of God?

IV. Do I keep holy the Lord's day, not only by refraining from common labor, but by endeavouring to derive, for myself and others, due religious improvement from its blessed privileges?

V. Do I discharge to those of my own family the obligations which I owe to them, not "grudgingly, as of necessity," but from the fulness of the heart? In the relations I sustain as son or daughter, brother or sister, husband or wife, father or mother, and in whatever other position I may be placed, how does conscience bear witness to my faithfulness?

VI. Have I sought to do injury, or wished evil, to any? Have I encouraged quarrels, or striven to appease them? Has my influence been, as far as I could exert any, on the side of peace and of the welfare of mankind?

VII. Have I been pure, not only in outward deed, but in word and thought? Do I exercise a rigid self-control, and refuse to indulge unduly any appetite or passion?

VIII. Do I sacredly respect the rights of others? Is my hand pure from all dishonest gains? Do I render unto all their dues, not only as required by law, but by the strictest judgment of conscience?

IX. Am I careful to guard against the sin of slander? Do I avoid the repetition of reports that are unfavorable to others, and discourage the propensity to circulate such reports where I perceive it in those around me? Do I ever, for convenience, or from a love of exaggeration, deviate from the plain rule of truth?

X. Am I contented with the blessings God has given, or is mine a restless, repining, envious spirit? Can I bear to see myself excelled by others? Do I covet my neighbour's goods, or see with pleasure the enjoyments which others receive from the Benefactor of all?

To these questions, derived from the ancient

Law, let me add the thoughts suggested by the more comprehensive summary of the Saviour. Matthew xxii. 37–40.

Is it my earnest wish to love the Lord my God with all my heart, and with all my soul, and with all my mind? Have I attained to any adequate degree of this holy feeling? How may I advance therein?

Do I love my neighbour as myself? Does the desire of doing good to others spring up within me as an ever-flowing fountain? Does my life, in all the relations I sustain, as a member of a family, as a citizen, as a man, bear witness to the existence of this principle within?

Do I observe the golden rule, doing unto others as I would that they should do unto me?

On these questions let me pause, and bring to memory my past conduct, especially of late. Then, having discerned wherein I am most deficient, let me address to my Heavenly Father a prayer of penitence.

PRAYER AFTER SELF-EXAMINATION.

O Thou who art of purer sight than to behold iniquity! how shall I come before thee, conscious as I am of many departures from thy law? As I survey my own past conduct, and compare it with the requirements of thy Divine commands, I feel that I have indeed come short of that obedience which it was my duty to render. I have yielded to unworthy motives; I have neglected duty; I have walked in forbidden paths. O God! grant me to feel, still more, my own unworthiness. Yet, O Thou whose property it is always to have mercy! grant, I pray thee, thy Divine forgiveness. I repent of my sins, and resolve to use my best endeavours to avoid them in future. May my repentance be accepted before thee, for I desire to present it in all lowliness and sincerity of heart. Do thou, O God! by the aid of thy holy spirit, render it more worthy of thine own acceptance.

May it be deep and permanent. May I be aided by thee, in the efforts on which I now resolve, to amend my outward conduct, to keep a guard over my lips, to restrain even my thoughts from evil. For my past offences, what satisfaction can I bring? I can but implore, in deep humility, thy forgiveness, and plead the promises of thy love, declared by Jesus Christ our Saviour. In the holy name of him who lived and died for man, I present my prayer unto thee, O Father! ascribing to thee infinite power, wisdom, love, and mercy. Amen.

PRAYER BEFORE COMMUNION.

O God, our Heavenly Father! thou didst, in infinite love, send thy well-beloved Son, Jesus Christ, our Lord, to lead mankind back from the mazes of sin, to the knowledge and love of thee, and the peace that is found in obedience. I thank thee for the precious blessings conferred through him. I thank thee for thy mercy to a world that lay in darkness and in sin. With deeper emotions, O God, do I bless thee for thy mercy displayed toward myself individually. Thanks to thee, O Father! that I have had my birth and education in a Christian land; thanks for the instructions with which I have been favored, whether in early youth or in riper years, that have contributed to keep me from sin, and to lead me in the way in which I ought to tread. Thanks to thee for the means of grace afforded me, in the privileges of public worship, and in the ordinances of the Gospel. With shame do I confess that my conduct has not been conformable, in all respects, to the advantages I have enjoyed. It is not of my own merit, but of thy mercy, that I am permitted to draw nigh to thee, and encouraged to share in the memorials of my Saviour's dying love. O God! may it be with deep humility that I unite with my fellow-believers in this affecting ordinance. May no feeling of spiritual pride arise within me, but rather may I realize that new and increased effort is needed, that I may hold my profession unstained and be steadfast unto the end. And for those with whom I unite, I pray as for myself. Aid us, O God! to contemplate with heartfelt gratitude the self-sacrificing love of our holy Redeemer. Aid us to meditate upon the perfections of his character, and to derive thence light to discern, and strength to pursue, our own path of duty. And unto thee, O God! as an humble disciple of that blessed Saviour, do I ascribe the kingdom, the power, and the glory, for ever. Amen.

PRAYER BEFORE COMMUNION, IN PROSPERITY.

O God, Bestower of every blessing! I give thanks to thee for the love that has crowned my days. Thy mercies are more than I can number. Let my heart with gratitude acknowledge them; let my life show forth that this gratitude is sincere. And now, O Father, as I am about to "take the cup of salvation, and call upon the name of the Lord," — to "pay my vows unto thee, in the presence of thy people,"— grant that I may bring to the hallowed ordinance those thoughts and feelings that are appropriate. Keep far from me that pride which would ascribe to myself the blessings I enjoy. I have nothing but what I have received from thee; whether health, or friends, or possessions, all are thine. May I feel this ever, and now especially, as I commemorate him who, "though he were rich, yet for our sakes became poor, that we through his poverty might be rich." May I so far as is in my power imitate his holy example, using the means thou hast bestowed upon me, not for my own good only, but as thy steward, for the good of those around me. Keep me, O Lord, safe from the trials which beset a prosperous condition; from pride and vanity, from the love of selfish indulgence, from neglect of the claims of my fellow-beings, from indifference to their sufferings, from forgetfulness of thyself, and disregard of thy holy law. And thine for ever, O God, be praise and glory in the highest, in the name of Jesus Christ, our Lord. Amen.

PRAYER BEFORE COMMUNION, IN ADVERSITY.

THOU givest, O God! life and all life's blessings; and when thou dost resume them, still blessed be thy holy name for ever! I come, O Father! bowed low by affliction, to discharge my duty, and seek for comfort and strength, in commemorating him who tasted the cup of sorrow for my sake. O, grant me grace to contemplate aright the perfections of his character; to feel that, if he so meekly and patiently endured, it becomes me, as his disciple, to bear thy holy will without a murmur. May I be encouraged by the thought, that, as thy Divine purposes for man's redemption were wrought out by the sufferings of Jesus, so every burden that we are called to bear will become, if patiently endured, the means for the accomplishment of some wise and gracious design. Send me, O Lord! if it seem fit to thee, relief from the trial under which I am placed. But more fervently would I pray thee, increase my faith and my patience to bear it. I bless thee for whatever circumstances of relief or comfort thou hast afforded, and for the many mercies to which the course of my life bears witness. Enable me more fully to realize thy goodness, in the past and in the present. Suffer not my strength to fail, O God! but may I sustain my trials and discharge my duties as befits an humble disciple of the blessed Jesus. And to thee, in his holy name, be praises for evermore. Amen.

PRAYER BEFORE COMMUNION, WHEN PRIVATELY ADMINISTERED IN SICKNESS.

O Thou in whose hands our life and breath are! I bless thee that before I am called hence, to be no more seen on earth, thou dost permit me to commemorate my Saviour in the way of his appointment. Thine hand is upon me, and I cannot go with the multitude of them that keep holy day, to meet my Redeemer and my God in the house of prayer. But thou preparest for me, here in privacy, the table of thine outward ordinance. O, nourish my longing spirit with heavenly food. As in these emblems I behold the death of my Saviour, let me derive from the contemplation strength for the scene that perhaps ere long awaits myself. May his meek endurance be reflected in mine. May his constant faith, his submission to thy holy will, his love to thee, to his disciples and friends, and to all mankind, produce in me their own resemblance. If I have cherished thus far an unkind feeling toward any, enable me now, O God! to banish it for ever from my breast, as I think of him who prayed for thy forgiveness on his murderers. If the pains of my sickness are severe, let my thoughts rest on those of my Redeemer's cross; and wilt thou, O Father! who didst strengthen him in the sorrows of Gethsemane, sustain me in the anticipation and in the reality of that which is before me. Grant, O Lord! that I may part from life with calm and perfect trust in thee. I have sinned; forgive thou my sins; confirm, perfect, and accept my penitence. And when death is past, O Father! shall I then — rapturous thought! — enter into the bliss reserved for those who are found faithful? Why should I fear, when this is before me? Fulfil, O my God! the blessed anticipation, and to thee, in the hallowed name of the Sufferer on Calvary, be glory ascribed, now, and with my dying voice. Amen.

PASSAGES OF SCRIPTURE.

God so loved the world, that he gave his only begotten Son, that whosoever believeth in him should not perish, but have everlasting life. John iii. 16.

Scarcely for a righteous man will one die; yet peradventure for a good man some would even dare to die. But God commendeth his love toward us, in that while we were yet sinners, Christ died for us. Romans v. 7, 8.

For it became him, for whom are all things, and by whom are all things, in bringing many sons unto glory, to make the Captain of their salvation perfect through sufferings. Heb. ii. 10.

For such an high-priest became us, who is holy, harmless, undefiled, separate from sinners, and made higher than the heavens. Heb. vii. 26.

Christ also suffered for us, leaving us an example, that ye should follow his steps: who did no sin, neither was guile found in his mouth: who, when he was reviled, reviled not again; when he suffered, he threatened not; but committed himself to him that judgeth righteously: who his own self bare our sins in his own body on the tree, that we, being dead to sins, should live unto righteousness: by whose stripes ye were healed. 1 Peter ii. 21–24.

Behold my servant, whom I uphold; mine elect, in whom my soul delighteth; I have put my spirit upon him: he shall bring forth judgment to the Gentiles. He shall not cry, nor lift up, nor cause his voice to be heard in the street. A bruised reed shall he not break, and the smoking flax shall he not quench: he shall bring forth judgment unto truth. Isaiah xlii. 1–3; Matt. xii. 17–20.

Then spake Jesus again unto them, saying, I am the light of the world: he that followeth me shall not walk in darkness, but shall have the light of life. John viii. 12.

Come unto me, all ye that labor, and are heavy laden, and I will give you rest. Take my yoke upon you, and learn of me: for I am meek and lowly in heart: and ye shall find rest unto your souls. For my yoke is easy, and my burden is light. Matt. xi. 28–30.

Behold the Lamb of God, which taketh away the sin of the world! John i. 29.

I am the good shepherd: the good shepherd giveth his life for the sheep. John x. 11.

Surely he hath borne our griefs, and carried our sorrows. He was wounded for our transgressions, he was bruised for our iniquities; the chastisement of our peace was upon him; and with his stripes we are healed. All we like sheep have gone astray; we have turned every one to his own way; and the Lord hath laid on him the iniquity of us all. He was oppressed, and he was afflicted, yet he opened not his mouth: he is brought as a lamb to the slaughter, and as a sheep before her shearers is dumb, so he opened not his mouth. Isaiah liii. 4–7.

This is my commandment, that ye love one another, as I have loved you. Greater love hath no man than this, that a man lay down his life for his friends. Ye are my friends, if ye do whatsoever I command you. John xv. 12–14.

Whosoever shall do the will of my Father which is in heaven, the same is my brother, and sister, and mother. Matt. xii. 50.

Herein is love, not that we loved God, but that he loved us, and sent his Son to be the propitiation for our sins. Beloved, if God so loved us, we ought also to love one another. God is love;

and he that dwelleth in love dwelleth in God, and God in him. 1 John iv. 10, 11, 16.

Christ our passover is sacrificed for us; therefore let us keep the feast, not with old leaven, neither with the leaven of malice and wickedness; but with the unleavened bread of sincerity and truth. 1 Cor. v. 7, 8.

Friend, how camest thou in hither, not having a wedding garment? Matt. xxii. 12.

Why call ye me, Lord, Lord, and do not the things which I say? Luke vi. 46.

Let your light so shine before men, that they may see your good works, and glorify your Father which is in heaven. Matt. v. 16.

Blessed are the pure in heart, for they shall see God. Blessed are the peace-makers, for they shall be called the children of God. Matt. v. 8, 9.

He that taketh not his cross, and followeth after me, is not worthy of me. Matt. x. 38.

Now the end of the commandment is charity, out of a pure heart, and of a good conscience, and of faith unfeigned. 1 Tim. i. 5.

Denying ungodliness and worldly lusts, we should live soberly, righteously, and godly in this present world; looking for that blessed hope, and the glorious appearing of the great God and our Saviour Jesus Christ; who gave himself for us, that he might redeem us from all iniquity, and purify unto himself a peculiar people, zealous of good works. Titus ii. 12–14.

Beloved, now are we the sons of God, and it doth not yet appear what we shall be: but we know that, when he shall appear, we shall be like him, for we shall see him as he is. 1 John iii. 2.

PART IV.

THE CHRISTIAN'S WALK.

PART IV.

THE CHRISTIAN'S WALK.

BEARING THE CROSS.

"He that taketh not his cross, and followeth after me, is not worthy of me." — Matt. x. 38.

It was not without reason that our Lord prepared the minds of his disciples, by such words as these, for the exercise of self-denial, and the endurance of suffering. The fulfilment of their duty to him and to his cause required of them, in that age, no slight amount of firmness, no wavering faith nor lukewarm zeal. The first requirement was indifference to worldly property, and, on the part of the teachers of the religion, its relinquishment. This was necessary, in order that their minds might undividedly attend to the one great object to which they were to be devoted. The scorn and hatred of the community at large, and especially of the most respected and influential class, they were sure to incur. Toil and privation, the alienation of families and friends, imprisonments, scourgings and tortures, were consequences neither remote nor improbable, to the view of any who should avow themselves disciples of Jesus; and it was soon found, after the great Master himself had suffered, that they who aspired to follow him must prepare themselves for the probability of being called to glorify him by a martyr's death. Such were the crosses which the early disciples bore; and he who was not ready to bear them was declared unworthy of his Master.

Though times have changed, and persecution has ceased, the Gospel of Christ remains the same. It still requires the disciple to take up his Saviour's cross and follow him. Our devotion to his cause must be as entire, if we would be counted worthy of our Lord, as was that of those who went before us. If times of persecution should return, it cannot be questioned that our duty would be the same with that of those who suffered for Christ in the age which followed his ascension, — to bear, if need should be, the literal cross, or to endure whatever tortures a Herod or a Nero could devise, rather than forsake our Master or dishonor our faith. There is not less, then, of the spirit of faithful endurance in the heart required now than of old; but our more indulgent lot has placed us where the occasions for its exertion are less terrible. We have still to bear meekly and firmly whatever burden it may please Providence to impose; but Providence grants to us lighter burdens than were endured by those of old. Shall we not thankfully receive and faithfully sustain them?

We have, however, our crosses; and it is well for us that we have them. Well did that noble-hearted Christian, William Penn, place the sentiment as the title to one of his treatises, "No cross, no crown." It was by endurance that the Saviour was glorified; it is only by endurance, by meekly sustaining sorrow, and bravely combating with temptation, that we can rise to the resemblance of our Lord, to that perfection in holiness which shall be the crown of our everlasting rejoicing.

What, then, are our crosses? What is it that in this day the Christian must nerve himself to bear, faithfully and patiently, under the alternative of being declared unworthy of his Master? It is, first, in general terms, whatever affliction or trial Providence may send. Our sorrows come not now, as in ancient times, except in small proportion, as the direct consequence of our profession of Christianity. But we may still regard them as the cross we are to bear for Christ. He came, not only to strengthen the martyr to endure his fiery trial, but to minister aid in every form of suffering that man can know; and there are sometimes sufferings in common, modern, and outwardly peaceful life, which may well compare with those of martyrdom.

> "The writhings of a wounded heart
> Are fiercer than a foeman's dart.
> Oft in life's stillest shade reclining,
> In desolation unrepining,
> Without a hope on earth to find
> A mirror in an answering mind,
> Meek souls there are, who little dream
> Their daily strife an angel's theme,
> Or that the rod they take so calm
> Shall prove in heaven a martyr's palm."
>
> *Keble.*

There are some of our crosses, and those of the heaviest kind, sin alone excepted, in enduring which we have peculiarly the encouraging thought that we are following our Master. They are the very burdens which he bore before us. Such are poverty, labor, pain, disgrace, bereavement, temptation. Let us contemplate them in turn.

Poverty.—The Son of God, the Saviour of

men, had not where to lay his head. His subsistence while engaged in the work of his ministry was from the contributions of others. "Though he were rich, yet for our sakes he became poor, that we through his poverty might be rich." Few in our happy country are called to know the extreme of poverty, as endured by thousands in the Old World. Ours is more generally that middle station, which is as far removed from penury as from wealth; the condition for which one prayed of old, — "Give me neither poverty nor riches; feed me with food convenient for me; lest I be full, and deny thee, and say, Who is the Lord? or lest I be poor, and steal, and take the name of my God in vain." Proverbs xxx. 8, 9. Shall we not only fail to appreciate the moral advantages of such a position, but, when so much is granted, ungratefully complain that we have not more? Nay, rather, even if our lot be still more lowly, let us remember the poverty of Jesus, and reflect that "the disciple is not above his master, nor the servant above his lord."

Labor. — The ministry of Christ was not one of ease. The days were spent in journeying with his disciples, until, wearied with his travel, he rested, as by the well of Samaria; or in instructions to the multitude, who thronged upon him so continually, that at one time we are told he had not an interval "so much as to eat," and his own relatives went forth and sought to lay hold on him, "for they said he is beside himself." His nights were spent, in various instances, in retirement on some mountain height, where by prayer and meditation he was strengthening himself for still further endurance. If labor is in this world our portion, shall we not learn from his cross to endure ours?

Pain. — How many a Christian, suffering the agony of sickness, has turned in thought to those pains of body which the Redeemer endured, and found strength to bear as Christ had borne. When the weight of the literal cross was placed upon him, his frame was yet suffering under cruel inflictions, and as with toil he moved on beneath his burden, even the savage executioners so far compassionated him, as to compel another to assist him in sustaining it. Hence how short was the interval to the infliction of still more excruciating tortures, the completion of the horrid penalty which impious man exacted from the innocent and the holy! Yes! Let those who are called to endure pain think on the agonies of the Saviour's crucifixion, and learn patience of him who there so meekly suffered.

Disgrace. — Harder to bear than corporeal pain,

to a mind possessing any thing of nobleness, is the scorn of fellow-beings. To be despised and rejected of men, the object of reproach to all around, — can any affliction transcend this? Yet this too the Redeemer endured. He was thus despised, thus rejected. This trial was added to the immediate sufferings of his cross, when they that passed by, wagging their heads, exclaimed, "He saved others, himself he cannot save," — when even his own chosen friends betrayed, abandoned, and denied him. Scarcely in this age can it be ours to suffer disgrace for the cross of Christ; and yet there is something which the minds of those who ought to be his disciples represent to themselves as partaking of this character. They fear the opinions of men, if they should venture to be known as religious. The offence of the cross has not, in their view, entirely ceased; and, honored as the Gospel is by thousands, they are still afraid of the supposed dishonor accompanying its profession. Let them recognize, rather, if they are called to endure shame for the name of Jesus, in this very shame the cross which Providence summons them to bear. Let them heed then his words who declared, "He that taketh not his cross, and followeth after me, is not worthy of me," and instead of shrinking from the light yoke and easy burden which the Gospel in this age presents, let them emulate the self-devoted spirit of those disciples, who returned from trial and scourging to give thanks, " rejoicing that they were counted worthy to suffer shame for his name." Acts v. 41.

Bereavement. — Painful is that trial, and it comes in turn to us all.

> " Friend after friend departs;
> Who hath not lost a friend?"

It is sad to bid the last farewell to those we love. Whether they go from us in infancy, in middle life, or in age, whether the blow be sudden or long anticipated, we feel that grief must have way, that nature bids us lament; nor can religion, with all her consolations, prevent our rendering the tribute of sorrow which affection claims. Yet, Christian, in thy mourning, feel thou that the cross thou bearest is that which Providence hath imposed upon thee; — feel, too, and be consoled by the remembrance, that he in whose steps thou art treading bore this cross also. Jesus, like thee, wept by a friend's grave. Hallowed remembrance! What Christian has mourned and has found consolation, that would bear to lose from the Scriptures that passage in which the beloved disciple has recorded the tears of Jesus by the grave of Lazarus? In another sense, too, did Jesus endure bereavement. Who ever was, like him, alone among mankind? His nearest friends could not comprehend his spirit nor his purposes. His disciples, at the moment of danger, "forsook him and fled."

Temptation. — Grievous are the sufferings of bodily anguish, sharp the pangs of a lacerated spirit; but there is a cross more to be dreaded than these. It is temptation. Better the death of the body than the ruin of the soul; and temptation is that which threatens the soul's ruin. The Saviour himself taught his disciples to pray, "Lead us not into temptation"; and yet we have to tread that path; we know that we must tread it so long as life remains. Our position is one of struggle against evil inducements; and the Divine wisdom sees best, for reasons which we can partially discern, that it should be so. But despair not, disciple of Jesus, who bearest the cross of temptation; for he also bore it, and bore it triumphantly. From the first hours of his ministry, when, led by the spirit into the wilderness to meditate, he beheld the prizes of ambition placed before him, and turned from them all to follow the straight and narrow path of duty, through all his long course of faithfulness, up to the hour when he bore meek yet majestic witness to the truth before

Pontius Pilate, did he "suffer, being tempted." How hard that trial was, it is in some instances permitted us to have an idea from the expressions which it wrung from him. "Pray," said he to his disciples once after such an inward contest, — "pray that ye enter not into temptation; the spirit truly is willing, but the flesh is weak." "Now," he said at another time, — "now is my soul troubled, and what shall I say? Father, save me from this hour? But for this cause came I unto this hour. Father, glorify thy name!" Temptation could assail him, but it could not conquer. Firmly he endured that cross also, and having remained faithful unto death, he is set down at the right hand of the Majesty on high. Let the tempted look to Jesus, and since the cross of trial is appointed by God, firmly, though in humility, assume, and resolutely bear it, remembering that Jesus thus sustained it, who was tempted in all points as we are, yet without sin.

Coinciding more or less nearly with one or another of these classes of endurance which we have now glanced at, are the various crosses which individuals are called to bear. Generally, too, there is to each one some peculiar cross, which he may recognize as being the evil he most desires to have removed, or the want which he most wishes to have gratified. And the thought may sufficiently indicate how such trials are to be borne, that the very earnestness of his wish may serve to show him what that is, the endurance of which is at the time the very cross that Providence imposes on him; patience under it the very duty which at that moment his God requires. Is labor hard to you? Then that labor is your cross, by meekly bearing which you can follow your Saviour. Do you feel that you could with pleasure endure labor, but pine at the confinement of your sick-room, which forbids you to engage in it? Be comforted, then, by the feeling, that the service of God is as possible to you now as it was in the hours of health. Your peculiar cross is now sickness; — your peculiar duty, to bear it resignedly. When recovery comes, be thankful, but expect not that in the removal of one cross your service is ended. Still there will be something to endure; and you, if you are a faithful Christian, would not have it otherwise, — would not be found unmarked with that sacred sign, which the Redeemer bore, and which his true followers must bear.

There is one cross which it is ours to bear, that, unlike those which have been named, was not endured by Christ. It is sin. Yes; we must bear what our Saviour never bore, the consciousness of neglected opportunities, duties unperformed, and transgressions committed. We must endure the trial of those temptations which derive increase of strength from our own previous criminal yielding to them; ours must be the shame and the agony of regret. Far better any other suffering than this; yet this, too, is a cross which we have a duty to perform in enduring. If we are guilty in the sight of God, the consciousness of that guilt is, with unquestionable justice, made a part of the burden we are to sustain; and in sustaining it is exercise for humility of spirit, for penitence which looks upon the past, and for holy determination which contemplates the future. We have to strengthen us the assurance that God is merciful, — yet more, that God is our Father. But for this, the cross of sin would be intolerable. Let us not shrink, then, from the contemplation of past errors. It is a part of the duty we owe to Him who in all but his sinlessness was our brother; it is a cross, though not like his, which, if endured aright, may be the means of making us resemble him more perfectly, by the power of true repentance to win back the forfeited brightness of innocence.

INSTRUMENTAL AND ACTIVE DUTIES.

The duties of the communicant, it is sufficiently obvious, are essentially the same which are incumbent upon all. Our obligations to God and to our fellow-men do not depend on our acknowledging their existence. The law of Christ is the rule of life prescribed for us by Divine authority, and our neglect of one among its precepts surely does not excuse us from obedience to the others.

Still it is true, that every right action we perform gives a pledge of consistent action in future; and that a falling into sin involves more of disgrace, and more of moral injury to ourselves and others, the higher our characters have previously stood. To ourselves, there is danger that the greatness of the fall may produce discouragement, instead of salutary penitence; and those who behold are liable to be hardened in sin, and tempted to disbelieve and scorn the power of virtue and religion. The offences of professed disciples "give occasion to the enemies of the Lord to blaspheme." The most mournful wounds which religion has received have been "in the house of her friends."

The believer, then, who in a sincere and humble spirit has joined the Church of Christ, cannot be indifferent to the question, What course of life should I pursue, that it may be consistent with the profession that I have made? What duties are yet before me, and how am I to discharge them?

The duties of the Christian's life may be classified under the divisions of instrumental, passive, and active. Of these, the second class has already received our notice, in the preceding section. The instrumental and the active duties remain for us to consider.

Under the former may be named the reading of the Scriptures, self-examination, and prayer, together with the observance of the Lord's day and its ordinances. These are means for improvement in actual virtue; they are instruments for cultivating within us the love of God and man.

Let not any one fancy that the advancement he has already made justifies him in neglecting the duties of personal religion. Let not any one fancy that a profession once made of faith in Christ is enough to make him and keep him a religious man. Religion is not a thing once to be experienced and afterwards to be left to itself. The mind and heart require nourishment, as much as the body. As the human frame without food would languish and die, so without inward, spiritual food, the soul languishes, the spiritual powers are weakened, the religious character dies.

And what is this food of the soul? How is the immortal spirit to be sustained? Prayer, reading, reflection, self-examination, the services of God's house, and active virtue, — these are the means of sustaining that religious character which is the soul's life. And though active virtue be of the list, let it not be thought that the others can safely be relinquished. Nor are prayer and reflection to be dreaded or shunned. To the pious mind, they are among the highest pleasures. Sometimes, indeed, it is painful to reflect, — it is painful even to pray, — when reflection finds no theme but the remembrance of lost opportunities and committed faults, and when prayer is the pleading of a spirit that is struggling to be humble, but has not yet fully attained the humility which makes prayer delightful. But when sin and pride are yielding,— when we can trace in our own characters something of improvement,— when we can indulge a hope that we are somewhat nearer heaven than before, and when, at the same time, we have so far conquered the temptation to vanity and self-admiration, as to recognize God, and not ourselves, as the author of this advancement,— then, indeed, reflection is pleasure; and prayer is the spontaneous and delighted pouring forth of gratitude to Him whose presence we feel to be around us, and whose grace we feel to be in our hearts.

But it is not only at such times that the Christian is to pray, or read, or meditate. It is a fatal mistake of some, to think they need only attend to these duties when their inclination prompts. They say, that sometimes, when their devotional feelings are excited, they do pray,— sometimes, when so disposed, they do read the Scriptures. This is leaving their religion to be the result of accident. What is postponed now for want of suitable feeling, now again for want of time, may soon be entirely neglected. Whatever is worth doing at all is worth doing regularly, at stated intervals. And at these intervals, if the mind is not in a right train for the service, it is to be brought into a right train. Reflection can be called up, to remind us how great is the Being in whose presence we stand, our God, the Lord of heaven and earth, the Eternal, Invisible, Unsearchable God, whom no mortal eye can see, and who yet is around us constantly, who sees all our actions, hears every word, and traces every thought, though it be almost hidden from ourselves. Thus can the mind be suitably composed for the high intercourse of prayer; and if devotion does not ascend on her boldest wing, at least the exercise will be an offering of such as we have to offer, and our spirits will be, by its influence, in some degree purified and elevated. Let prayer, then, and reading, reflection and self-examination, be made regular duties.

The hours of morning and of evening are suggested by nature, by Scripture, and by the common consent of mankind, as the suitable seasons for regular devotion. And what is the most appropriate period for self-examination? This is, indeed, like prayer, a duty for all times and places. The individual must ever have a watch over himself, and must ever be ready, even though amidst a crowd, to seek, in silent ejaculation, aid from heaven. But as for prayer, so also for self-examination, the allotment of some definite period of time is the best way to insure the regular performance of the duty. The calm leisure of the Sabbath day, the recurrence of the ordinance commemorative of our Saviour, and whatever periods of the year are hallowed to our recollection by events of peculiar importance,—these may well be employed for the purpose of a self-communion, in which conscience shall penetrate the recesses of the soul, and dislodge thence every bad passion, every unholy thought, every guest unworthy to endure the presence of that God to whom we have consecrated the temple of the heart.

Among the means which we may use for our own improvement and the expression of reverence to God, are some which are also to be classed among our duties to others. Such are family prayer, public worship, and the use of the ordinances of religion.

Family prayer, where properly conducted, is the blessing of God on the domestic circle. We will not say merely that it calls down a blessing, though this we believe; but it is in itself a blessing. It introduces, more than can in any other way be done, the spirit of religion into the circle of parents and children, brothers and sisters. It binds all together with the golden chain of love to one another, and to the Father and to the Saviour of all. To the younger portion of the family its influence may be most valuable. The example of the parent is set before them as a motive to personal religion; and no motive can be more powerful. Is it objected, that few are competent to conduct the exercise in an appropriate manner? We may reply, that excellent manuals of devotion are accessible to all; and that it is not in the number of words that the influence of family prayer consists, but in the act of the domestic circle uniting each day to acknowledge the goodness and to seek the blessing of God. Of the direct answer that is granted to such prayers, there seems no further reason to doubt, than of the answer to public or to individual supplications. We know that the Scriptures authorize and inculcate prayer; that the patriarchs worshipped in the presence of their families, and the Saviour among his disciples. We doubt not that our devotions are known to the Omniscient; nor that the All-merciful and All-powerful is equally willing and able to bestow the blessings that are suitably implored.

Next to family worship, attendance on the services of the sanctuary presents itself for our reflection. This, like the discharge of the other instrumental duties of religion, should be regular. We have already laid down the principle, that whatever object is to be accomplished can be better effected by systematic efforts, than by regarding merely the promptings of occasional inclination. And let us remember, that our Saviour enforced the precept, "Take heed how ye hear." Let us remember that he compared the preaching of the Gospel to the scattering of seed, which fell in vain, unless it fell on good ground; and that even of those who attended on his preaching, the greater number, from want of due preparation on their own part, derived no advantage from their inestimable privilege. Hence may we learn to bring to the house of prayer the hearing ear, the understanding heart, and the docile and obedient spirit.

With respect to the employment of those hours of the Lord's day which are not spent in public worship, we may observe, in general terms, that he who wishes to derive real improvement from the thoughts presented to him in church will not be disposed to engage immediately after in any thing, either of business or of pleasure, which would banish every serious thought from his mind. "The Sabbath was made for man"; but much of its usefulness to man depends upon his holding it sacred, — sacred from the common cares of life, and from some of its ordinary enjoyments. Enjoyments the day may and ought to have. It should be, it is meant to be, the happiest day of all the seven. But its pleasures should be of that quiet, simple, thoughtful character, that may be consistent with the serious duties that engage a portion of its hours. And in regard even to occupations which may appear in themselves innocent, the Christian, if he has the spirit of his Master and of Paul, will be disposed rather to deny himself than to do "any thing whereby a brother may stumble, or be led into sin, or be made weak." Rom. xiv. 21.

Thus have we reviewed the instrumental duties of religion, with the exception of the Lord's Supper itself. In this the disciple will engage in deference to the command of his Saviour, and not in deference to that alone. He will strive to cultivate within himself that spirit of love to his Master, which will render participation in the memorial of his Master's death, not merely a duty, but a pleasure. He will regard the communion as a proper occasion for self-inspection, and for a renewed examination of the perfect character of his Saviour. Prayer and praise are sacred to our God; the communion is sacred to Jesus Christ, not as an act of worship, but of friendly, brotherly commemoration.

But the Supper of the Lord, like public, social, and private prayer, though valuable in itself, will be by such a person valued most as instrumental to something beyond. He will remember the solemn meaning of those words, "Let every one that nameth the name of Christ depart from iniquity." (2 Tim. ii. 19.) He will feel that the discharge of duty to man is the mode of service most acceptable to that God who declared of old, "I will have mercy, and not sacrifice."

"Ye," said our Saviour to his disciples, "ye are the salt of the earth"; "ye are the light of the world." These are lofty titles; but they were applied by our holy Master to the band of his followers, and to the band of his followers they still belong. The Christian Church is now, as of old, the salt of the earth, the light of the world. The members, then, of the Christian Church should remember the influence they exert, and their responsibleness for its exercise. If the salt have lost its savor, wherewith shall it be seasoned? If the light of the world become darkness, how great is that darkness!

Leaving the instrumental, we now approach the active duties of the Christian,—those which he is called upon to discharge toward his fellow-men. First among them we may with propriety notice what is due to his associates in the Church.

Communicants at present form among us a distinct body; and a distinct body they must form, until either the ordinance shall cease to be observed, — which we trust may never be, — or until all shall unite in it. However we may regret the distinction between church and congregation, we must act according to the existing state of things. Perceiving, then, that some of each religious society are peculiarly united together, if by no other tie, at least by meeting each other at the communion, we must consider what duties these owe to one another.

This point would be very differently settled in different assemblies of Christians. Among some, were we to propose this question, we should be told that each member of the Church owes it to his brethren to exercise a strict, though affectionate, watch over their conduct, freely though kindly to admonish them of any perceived error, and, if admonition should fail, to act in concert with the Church at large as a judicial tribunal for their examination and discipline. It must be confessed that this view of a church, as a body which is to exercise a very constant and watchful discipline over its members, is in accordance with the practice of the early Christians, and claims to be authorized by the precepts of our Saviour and the Apostles. But, on the other hand, it is to be remembered that the early Christians, living under a despotic and heathen government, had much more occasion for a tribunal within their own body, to compose their differences and pass censure on their faults, than exists at the present day. It is to be remembered that the experience of ages since that time has shown the great danger that attends the placing of temporal power in the hands of spiritual leaders. It is also worthy of remark, that our Saviour, if he laid down some principles of what may be called church discipline, pointed out in those principles a course of advice and remonstrance, not of coercion (Matt. xviii. 15, 17); and that the only instance in which St. Paul is recorded to have authorized even the suspension of a member from communion, was an instance of such gross immorality as not the most lenient church at the present day would tolerate. (1 Cor. v.; 2 Cor. ii.) Then, too, it may be urged with force, that a system of continual supervision of each other's conduct would be apt to do more harm, by the introduction of an inquisitive, intermeddling and suspicious spirit, than it could ever do good by the purifying effect of its discipline; that thus heart-burnings and jealousies would take the place of that brotherly love which ought to be the bond of Christian union; that in a community as numerous as Christian churches frequently are, there would often be persons who would combine a zeal for discipline with a narrowness of mind which would be unable to distinguish between matters of consequence and trifles, between forms and substance. Among the early Christians it was better to have points of difference concerning right subjected to the kind arbitration of their brethren, than decided by heathen judges. In the Dark Ages, when the right of the strongest often took the place of law and order, the spiritual weapons of suspension and excommunication, if they were often abused to wrong purposes, were perhaps still oftener valuable for right. But in our Christian and civilized age, it is better to leave questions that admit of such adjudication to be settled by the law of the land, to exercise church discipline only in extreme cases, for purging the Church from members whose lives would disgrace it, and to substitute in its stead a fraternal feeling among the members of the same communion, and an intercourse in which harmony shall be secured by mutual forbearance, and respect for the liberty of all.

It by no means follows, however, that those who meet at the same table to commemorate the death of their Lord, may not feel and encourage an interest in each other's welfare, or even that such an interest may not extend to the spiritual as well as temporal good of their fellow-members. Such an interest ought to exist. They who have fixed their hearts on the same object, they who are travelling the same road, should feel that they are indeed companions. It may often be in their power to facilitate each other's progress; to do so, should not be less a pleasure than a duty. Nor, while we find so many of the worthiest among us, who from various reasons decline attendance at the Communion, should we fail on this account to extend to them our fraternal sympathy and aid. The worshippers in the same house of prayer are bound together by a near and sacred relation. A relation less near, but not less sacred, connects together all the followers of the Saviour. Wherever we find a Christian, there should our hearts recognize a brother. It is said, that of old, when the professors of Christianity, few in number, were surrounded by a hostile world, the heathen, bitterly as they opposed them, could not avoid sometimes saying, "Behold, how these Christians love one another." Happy will be the Christian Church, if, at the present day, the same can be said;—and happy that portion of it, however small, in which unity of spirit, mutual respect, and brotherly kindness prevail.

What is the duty of the communicant toward the world at large? It differs in naught from the duty of any other member of society. It may naturally be expected, however, that the feelings which have led the disciple to a profession of religion will accompany him still, and shed the light of religious feeling and religious motive over every field of human obligation. In the constitution of society every man bears his part, but it often is the case that men are unacquainted with the true nature of the ties which bind them to each other. Prompted only by private interest or feeling, they discharge their part for the general good, and see not, all the time, that wisdom which has arranged the motives and course of their action. Each is like some inanimate portion of a machine, which yields blindly to the impulse of the moving power, unconscious of the purposes for which it is employed. Thus it is with men in every condition of life; alike with the tiller of the ground and with the conqueror; both are instruments in the hands of Providence, and Providence employs the one to aid in producing sustenance for mankind, and the other to execute judgment on the guilty, and salutary discipline on the erring among nations; but each, meanwhile, sees only himself and the circle of private motives by which he is influenced. Religion communicates to man a knowledge of his true position. It is then as if the machine could become conscious of the results it is destined to effect, and of their importance. The individual now sees the bearing of his own conduct on the happiness of those around him, and perceives himself to be a fellow-worker with God for the benefit of society. This idea it is which distinguishes the duty and the conduct of the religious man. His eye is opened to his own true position. He sees that, while he has thought of nothing but the acquisition of property, God has made use of the industry he has thus developed for the good of society. He sees that, while he has thought only of gratifying his own taste, he has, without intending it, gratified also that of others. He enters then cheerfully into the plans of infinite benevolence, as he begins to understand them. His conduct perhaps is the same, but its motives are different. He labors now, not only for himself, but in part for the sake of others, and in part from a feeling in harmony with the plans of his Creator. He sees

God in all, and all in God. Has he children? He not only provides for them from the instinctive principle which sways the animal, he not only cherishes them for his own gratification,—though this instinctive principle, and this gratification in the growth and progress of his children, are strengthened, not weakened, by the introduction of higher motives,—but he contemplates God as the wise author and disposer of the parental relation,—he sees himself intrusted with these objects from a higher power, and on this view of duty does he conduct himself towards them. And so of every relation he sustains. This it is, as the Apostle commands, to "do all to the glory of God";—to feel, in whatever we have to do, the relation which it bears to God, and to our duty as his subjects. The man who realizes the feelings we have endeavoured to describe and convey, views the world from an entirely different and more elevated point than the community at large. Of the thousands around him, each sees only his own limited part; but this man, while he sees his own part, sends a glance abroad over the whole, views it in its relations to God, and himself coöperates with God's designs concerning it to the best of his ability. Thus it is that the love of God leads to the love of man; that piety introduces true philanthropy; because, as we come nearer to our Heavenly Father, understand his character and will better, and love him more, we feel more as he feels, in reference to our fellow-men.

The present is peculiarly an age of philanthropic exertion. Plans of benevolence of the widest extent, and adapted to all the varied forms of human suffering, are offered to the attention of the community. To their claims the consistent Christian cannot be indifferent. His first attention is due to those immediately around him; the duties of the son or brother, husband or father, must first be discharged; then follow those of the friend, the neighbour, and the citizen. It must be his to relieve distress, to encourage virtuous conduct, to warn against vice, among those to whom his direct influence extends. But beyond this sphere he has duties. The love taught him by his Saviour is not less comprehensive than the world. Among the many plans for the relief of suffering, the restraint of wrong, the advancement of knowledge, civilization, and Christianity, he is to choose, calmly and justly, such as commend themselves to his approval, and come within his power of efficient coöperation. It cannot be his to have a part in all the good that is done among mankind. It may be best that he should concentrate his efforts on some one object in the wide field of Christian beneficence. If so, still let him be just to others. Their efforts, too, must be bounded, from the very nature of things. It is neither desirable nor possible that all other objects should be forsaken for that which has engaged his attention. Never let him condemn that which he has not examined; never let him judge the motives and the consciences of others. In his own chosen sphere let him labor, whether success be sent to encourage, or disappointment to prove him. It is not the amount of what he shall accomplish, but the sincere fidelity with which he labors, that shall gain him the approval of conscience and of God. As to the approbation of men, let him not seek for it, except in strict subordination to those higher aims. With humility, but with steadfastness, let him follow in the path which Jesus trod, and though it should conduct him to the cross, beyond the cross is the heavenly crown.

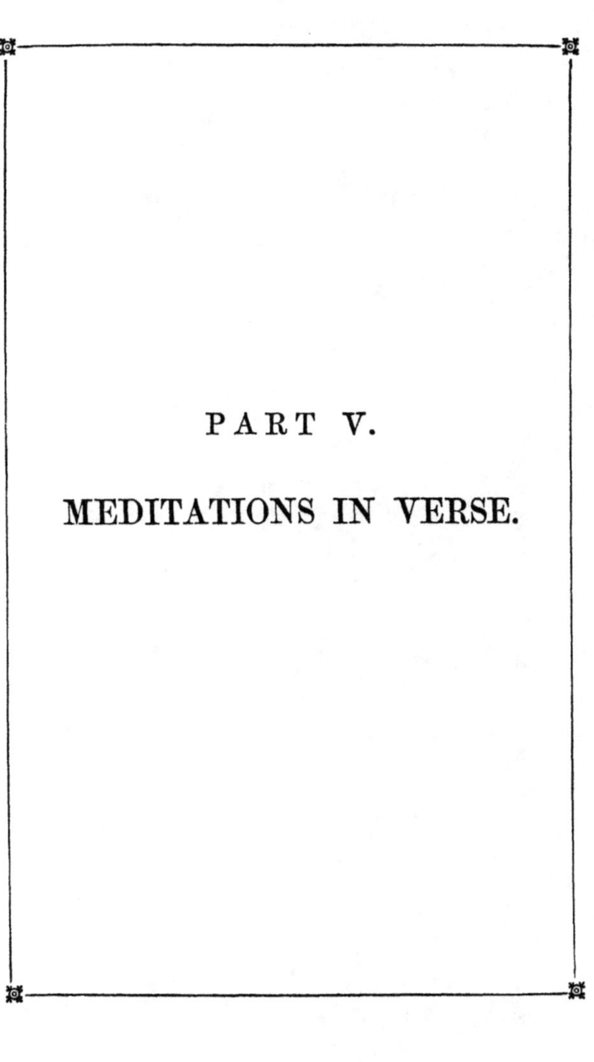

PART V.

MEDITATIONS IN VERSE.

PART V.

MEDITATIONS IN VERSE.

"BEHOLD THE MAN!"

BEHOLD the Man! By that calm eye,
  By that mild lip, my Lord I know;
But why those drops of crimson dye,
  That majesty of patient woe?

Around thee clings a robe of state,
  But ah! in mockery, stained and torn;
And for the crown's imperial weight,
  Thy temples bear the piercing thorn.

Behold the Man! Thy cheek is pale,
  Thy form with torture seems to faint;
But the strong soul can yet prevail,
  And the meek lip knows no complaint.

The wounds thy bleeding frame has borne,
  The sharper pangs thou yet must bear,

The princes' hate, the soldiers' scorn, —
  Are there worse ills than these to share?

Yes! it is worse to die abhorred
  By those whom thou hast lived to save,
To hear thine Israel doom her Lord,
  Her benefactor, to the grave.

Yet, Saviour, there were thoughts that came,
  Like angel ministrants, to cheer
Thy spirit through that pain and shame;
  And one among them, bright and dear; —

That coming ages should repay,
  By love, the scorn of that sad hour;
For visioned to thy spirit lay
  Thy rising kingdom's future power.

And now is that fruition thine
  Whose hope could then thy soul sustain;
And thou, enthroned in bliss divine,
  Art spreading still thy glorious reign.

Lo, heathen altars crumbling fall!
  Lo, ocean's isles thy voice obey!
And soon the light that beams for all,
  O'er the wide earth shall pour its ray.

And we, — shall not our spirits bend
  To him who in that strife o'ercame?
Our praises for that King ascend,
  Who comes in God his Father's name?

Yes, by that patient, bleeding brow,
  By all thy wrongs, by all thy love!
Saviour! before thee here we bow,
  Thy service be our bliss above!

JESUS BEFORE PILATE.

"Art thou a king?" O, not in vain
Those words, though meant in scorn;
For ne'er was captive monarch's chain
With more of grandeur worn.

"Thou sayest"; — the assent was given,
With calmness, not with pride;
Nor he, though loved and crowned of heaven,
That earthly power defied.

"My kingdom is not of this earth,
Else had my servants fought;
But consecrated from my birth,
For truth I've lived and taught;

"And hearts to whom the truth is dear
Are subjects of my throne.
My law they love, my voice they hear,
My gentle kingdom own."

"What, then, is truth?" the Roman cried,
Yet careless turned away,

Self-fated, darkling to abide,
So near the perfect day.

O King of truth! we bless thy sway,
Thy law would learn and love.
On earth conduct us in thy way,
And own us thine above!

THE CROWN OF THORNS.

A CROWN for the destined King!
The weight of gold by David borne,
From conquered Ammon torn!*
To David's heir the regal circle bring,
And let the ruby's rays
Join with the sapphire's blaze
To make for Judah's Lord an offering.

A crown for the gentle Friend,
Whose heart with human love o'erflows,
Who feels for human woes!
The rose and myrtle with the olive blend,
And let the mingled wreath
Each softest odor breathe,
And music's liquid melody attend.

A crown for the Lofty One!
For him who reigns in heavenly might,
Next to the Infinite!

* "And he took their king's crown from off his head, (the weight whereof was a talent of gold, with the precious stones,) and it was set on David's head." 2 Sam. xii. 30.

But what were worthy of God's holy Son,
  Unless night's diadem,
  With every starry gem,
By angel hands were laid before his throne?

  A crown of the piercing thorn
Was woven for that sacred brow,
  And lo! the soldiers bow,
And hail the meek Redeemer king, in scorn!
  Christian! there fix thy gaze!
  Nor gems nor starry rays
Equal the glories which that crown adorn.

"MY GOD! MY GOD! WHY HAST THOU FORSAKEN ME?"

Hast thou forsaken me?
Father and God! to thee
    Humbly I cry.
Free from temptation's thrall,
Loving and blessing all,
    Yet here I die.

Hast thou not said of old,
Thou wouldst my throne uphold
    Against all fear?
Hast thou not made, through me,
Blind eyes the light to see,
    Deaf ears to hear?

Has not my fervent prayer
Risen through midnight's air
    On the lone hill,
While, like the stars above,
Thine answering thoughts of love
    Burned calm and still?

Darkness around me lies!
Scarce can my spirit rise
O'er the sharp pain.
Thoughts of a world redeemed,
How brightly once ye beamed!
Beam yet again!

God! thou hast given me power
To brave this fearful hour;
Leave me not now!
Torn limbs and burning thirst!
Malice has done its worst!
Be near me thou!

THE MOURNERS.

The nails are loosened from the cross,
  And now the sacred form,
With bending head, like flower that bows
  Before the northern storm,
Received by friendly arms, is laid
  On yonder grassy mound,
While silently, in reverent grief,
  The mourners gather round.

And Roman proud and Pharisee
  At distance gaze with awe,
For sternest breasts confess at times
  Our nature's holy law.
They thought despair and baffled guilt
  Above that form would rave,
And stern-browed partisans would bear
  Their leader to his grave.

But lo! a woe-struck woman kneels
  To kiss that cheek of clay;
No tear her agony reveals,—
  It may not so find way.

O Mary! mother of the Lord!
  Are these cold limbs the same
With the bright infant's form, that erst
  By thee to being came?

Approach, O maid of Magdala,
  Once rescued by his grace,
And thou who at his sacred feet
  Hast held a happy place;
And thou, the true disciple, come!
  Where pierced that Roman spear
The heart is still, that beat for all,
  And thee, of all most dear.

Thou, who by night hast trembling sought
  To hear his hallowed word,
Fear'st not, new-born, in this sad hour,
  To own him for thy Lord.
And Joseph with thee ministers,
  To whom dark Pilate gave, —
While conscience blanched his war-stained cheek,—
  The body for the grave.

Weep! weep! yet upward let the gaze
  Of faith reviving turn;
The heavens that darkened o'er his cross
  With sunset's glory burn!
Trust, mourners, trust! Still reigns on high
  The God who loves the just;
He can bid life and glory bloom
  From hopes now laid in dust.

MARY AND JOHN, BEFORE THE RESURRECTION.

My mother! in the awful hour
When darkness o'er us lay,
While, fainting by the Blest One's cross,
My arm became thy stay,
Did not his gentle voice then seal
The bond for thee and me,
And give me for the coming time
To be a son to thee?

O privilege of all most high!
O boon of all most dear!
Still, still, in sweet, sad memory
That voice I seem to hear.
Then come, my mother! share the cot
Thy Jesus oft hath blest,
Far hence, where blue Gennesareth
Expands his peaceful breast.

The boat lies idle on the strand,
The net hangs by the wall;

In happier hour, when hope was high,
  For him I left them all.
Now, for his sake and thine, I turn
  Back to that quiet sea.
Farewell, ye proud and guilty towers!
  My mother! come with me!

There oft, when eve's advancing shades
  O'er hill and lake are thrown,
Will we recall the varied past,
  And weep for hopes now gone.
Then will we waken slumbering faith,
  And lift our brightening eyes
To Him, who e'en from this deep gloom
  Can bid the light arise.

Yes, we will trust! My thought retains
  Words of mysterious power
The Loved One spoke, as o'er his soul
  Darkened the destined hour.
That he should rise again! O joy!
  But ah! for hope too dear!
Some mystic meaning sure was there,
  That time shall render clear.

Perchance another, in his might,
  With burning words shall come,
And lead repentant Israel forth
  To mourn above his tomb.
Perchance his rising will be there
  Where we with him shall rise,
To meet the Father's smile of love,
  In yonder holy skies!

But now, the night in watching spent,
  How glorious breaks the day !
The sisters hasten to the tomb,
  The last sad rites to pay ;
And lo ! our brethren's scattered band
  Are gathering mournfully, —
All here, except that sacred form
  We never more may see !

ZEAL AND LOVE.

On, on, Crusaders, once again,
To Salem's trembling towers!
The Moslem ranks resist in vain
Your consecrated powers.
Spare not the unbelieving horde;
On, for the cause divine!
And soon the banner of the Lord
On Zion's height shall shine!
Cease your wild shouts! Once on this hallowed air
Rose from the cross the dying Saviour's prayer,
"Father, forgive!"

On patriots, in your country's might!
Her injured honor calls!
Before her vindicated right
The insulting foeman falls.
Taste the stern joy of battle's hour,
And let your standard wave
Above your country's conquering power,
Or shroud her slaughtered brave!
But ah! do deeds of blood his impress bear
Who uttered once, for Judah's race, the prayer,
"Father, forgive"?

The Church! By open foes beset
And treachery's hidden wile,
She bids her children trample yet
On error's serpent guile.
The anathema has slept too long;
Now let its thunders burst
On those who lead the unwary throng
To heresy accurst!
Yet pause; no sound on Calvary's mournful air
Rose to the throne of God, save that meek prayer,
"Father, forgive!"

Forward, ye champions of the age!
Plead for God's holy truth,
With all the strength of manhood sage,
The energy of youth!
To that abyss whence first they came
Drive back the brood of night!
With heart of steel, with tongue of flame,
Do battle for the right!
Yet, ere ye strive, list to your Master's prayer,
Breathed on the cross for those who placed him there,
"Father, forgive!"

THE PENITENT THIEF.

Can late repentance then repair
  The ruin of a life of crime? —
Eternal justice grant the prayer
  Breathed at the awful goal of time?

Can habit's chains at once be burst, —
  The guilt-stained soul at once be pure, —
Sin from her old dominion thrust,
  And peace and pardon rendered sure?

O miracle of sovereign grace!
  Yet who that grace shall dare reprove, —
Question, O God, thy righteous ways,
  Thy boundless power, thy saving love?

And humble faith has strength untold;
  And penitence, transforming might,
To turn sin's dross to heaven's pure gold,
  And the soul's darkness into light.

That faith, in suffering and in scorn,
  The guiltless Son of God could own,

And reverence, of repentance born,
  Viewed in the cross Messiah's throne.

The Saviour blest that dying prayer,
  And hope may rise, though near the tomb.
One pardon found, lest man despair;
  One only, lest he should presume!

PRAYING IN THE NAME OF CHRIST.

"Whatsoever ye shall ask the Father in my name, he will give it you." — John xvi. 23.

By the Saviour's prayer to thee
Poured upon the fatal tree,
    Lord! thy help we crave!
Save from passion's tyrant force, —
From the stings of dire remorse!
    God and Father, save!

Save from evil habit's power!
God! be thou our strength and tower,
    Thou our sun and shield!
May our souls to thee aspire,
And their unseen foes retire
    From the conquered field!

Save us in the evil days
When our earthly strength decays,
    And the couch is spread;
Anxious friends, with footstep light,
Watching through the mournful night
    Round our dying bed.

Thou who wast to Jesus nigh,
God and Father! hear our cry!
    In his name 't is poured.
He hath led us to thy throne;
Hear us through thy blessed Son,
    Our ascended Lord!

INVITATION.

COME to the sacred feast!
Come for the Saviour's sake!
With reverent joy let every guest
The hallowed rite partake.

Think not 't is earthly bread;
Think not 't is common wine.
Of the torn frame, the blood once shed,
Behold the mystic sign!

Here let the young draw nigh,
And give life's golden hours
To Him who bids eternity
Expand its roseate bowers.

And here let man's firm tread
And woman's step of grace
Approach the feast of Jesus, spread
Within the sacred place.

Here let the aged come,
Who long has served his God;

Who, calmly hopeful, toward the tomb
  Treads as his Saviour trod.

  Blest Jesus! be thou near!
  Thy spirit o'er us reign!
The perfect love that casts out fear
  In every soul remain!

  Father and God! we own
  Thy presence round us now.
May lives of holiness make known
  That thou hast blest our vow!

THE COMMUNION OF SAINTS.

We gather to the sacred board,
Perchance a scanty band;
But with us in sublime accord
What mighty armies stand!

In creed and rite howe'er apart,
One Saviour still we own,
And pour the worship of the heart
Before one Father's throne.

A thousand spires o'er hill and vale
Point to the same blue heaven;
A thousand voices tell the tale
Of grace through Jesus given.

High choirs, in Europe's ancient fanes,
Praise him, for man who died;
And o'er our boundless Western plains
His name is glorified.

Around his tomb, on Salem's height,
Greek and Armenian bend;

And through far Laplands' months of night
  The peasant's hymns ascend.

Are we not brethren? Saviour dear!
  Then may we walk in love,
Joint subjects of thy kingdom here,
  Joint heirs of bliss above!

PRAISE.

AUTHOR of every good,
Giving thy creatures food,
Thou bidd'st the ocean's flood
    To rise and fall!
'T is thy all-ruling might
Marshals the host of night;
Thy goodness infinite
    Beams over all.

Day speaketh unto day,
From morning's earliest ray
Till evening fades away,
    O God! of thee.
And when the night has spread
Her mantle overhead,
Then through the darkness dread
    Thine eye can see!

Wherever man is found,
Thy love that knows no bound
Still doth his path surround,
    Father divine!

Thou giv'st the bright spring hours,
Thou, summer's leafy bowers;
Fruits which the autumn showers,
All, all are thine!

But of thy varied store
None wins our praises more
Than the immortal lore
Jesus hath given.
All the bright gifts of earth
Cannot approach the worth
Of the celestial birth,
Heirship of heaven!

Thou from whom Jesus came!
Keep us from sin and shame!
Kindle a holy flame
Within each breast!
Beneath thy loving eyes
Still may our souls arise,
Till in thy own pure skies
With thee they rest!

THE END.

www.ingramcontent.com/pod-product-compliance
Lightning Source LLC
LaVergne TN
LVHW011209110826
845150LV00006B/1373

* 9 7 8 1 4 2 5 5 1 7 8 4 7 *